THE LITERATURE OF ENGLAND - VOLUME ONE

Heroes and Pilgrims
449-1485

SINGER/RANDOM HOUSE LITERATURE SERIES

THE LITERATURE OF ENGLAND - VOLUME ONE

Heroes and Pilgrims 449-1485

Julian L. Maline, James Berkley, *General Editors*

William Shurr

George L. Ariffe

Dictionary of Questions for Understanding Literature by Vernon Ruland

Random House, Inc.

New York

SINGER / RANDOM HOUSE LITERATURE SERIES

Contributing Editors to the Series

Dwight L. Burton
Marion T. Garretson
Lydia G. Goforth
Chloe A. Morrison
John W. Ragle
Vernon Ruland
Thomas J. Shanahan
John S. Simmons
Thomas J. Steele
David Stryker
Paul A. Thetreau
Jerry L. Walker

Manufactured in the United States of America

394–00379–9

4 5 B A 9 8 7 6 5 4 3

Preface

"The unexamined life is not worth living" —*Socrates*
"Literature is the criticism of life" —*Matthew Arnold*

As Greece in its heyday had its Socrates, foe of the "unexamined life," so England at the peak of its literary fame in the nineteenth century had its Matthew Arnold. Both Socrates and Arnold belonged to that small group of exceptionally talented men who themselves understand the cultural issues of their times and yet are also men of action enough to spend their lives prodding their contemporaries to an awareness of these issues. Socrates knew that a man must know himself and the manifold varieties of human experience, or find life impoverished indeed. For his part, Matthew Arnold was reinforcing Socrates in repeating a truth that has been at the center of civilization since the beginning, namely, that literature is important for man's understanding of himself.

It is our privilege, in the spirit of Socrates and Arnold, to examine in some detail the high points of more than twelve centuries of British literature. It is a body of literature the earliest monuments of which reflect life around the smoky campfires of the Heroic Age and the views and reflections man had upon the human situation even then. Times change. There are periods of progress and periods of decline. But throughout, the literature of England continues to reflect man's most thoughtful reactions to life about him.

Selections in *The Literature of England* have been arranged historically to show the continuity of English literary tradition. Each unit in the four volumes comprising the complete text begins with an introduction, defining for the student some of the broader aspects of cultural history that have shaped the artist and influenced his craft. The selections themselves, however, are offered without individual commentary, to allow the student to make his own analysis of each piece, unprejudiced by someone else's interpretation.

At the heart of any English program – indeed, at the heart of any valuable educational theory – is a recognition of the importance of careful and critical reading ability. Traditionally, this has been called rhetorical analysis; more recently it has been called explication. It is a method which enables students to approach a work of literature on its own terms, to understand its form and structure as the essence of a work, as the method by which the author's meaning has been expressed and is to be understood. Only after this structure has been grasped can any valid statements be made about the intentions of the author or the significance of his work. The "Dictionary of Questions for Understanding Literature" is an adaptation of this explication method designed specifically for this series.

Immediately following each selection is a small box of numbers referring to the "Dictionary of Questions." Teachers and students are encouraged to use the "Dictionary of Questions" freely and selectively, and not to rely too literally on the questions suggested. However, the suggested questions highlight what the editors believe to be the most important areas in each work. Examples of how these questions might be applied to a particular work are seen in the Models included in the texts. These Models illustrate how an alert student might answer the "Dictionary" questions. Students should read these Models carefully, not only for the information about the use of the "Dictionary" which they provide, but also for the insights into the selections which they reveal.

Each unit concludes with a few Problem Questions which draw together controversial themes and important background material within a single unit or joining a number of units. These questions are intended to stimulate habits of review, independent thinking, and mature discussion and compositional work.

The footnotes provide the pronunciation and/or information necessary to understand a particular historical allusion, proper name, or word given an archaic or singular meaning by the author. These notes are seldom used to give suggested interpretations, or the meanings of words that could be readily discovered in a dictionary. Whenever the student meets a word marked with a degree symbol (°), he should look up the word in his own dictionary. This kind of vocabulary work is far more meaningful than the memorization of lists of words out of context. The pronunciation symbols are those used in the *Random House Dictionary of the English Language,* Unabridged Edition.

Many criteria have influenced the selection of material for this edition of *The Literature of England.* The major criterion, however, has been the literary worth of each piece. More specifically, this has meant choosing pieces that represent the best work of major authors and, at the same time, exemplify outstanding literary characteristics of the period in which they were written. There has been no thought of catering to a soft education by excluding whatever demands concentrated and serious thought.

Lionel Trilling has spoken of literature as "the great traditional agency of real awareness." Should these literature texts produce in the students who use them a richer and more intelligent appreciation of this agency, its editors will have been amply rewarded.

Contents

Introduction

SETTING THE STAGE

The Land

The subject of our study is the literature produced on an island considerably smaller than the area covered by Ohio and Illinois, roughly half the size of California. Englishmen joke and tourists complain about its weather; Tacitus, the ancient Roman historian, was exaggerating only a little when he said "the sky is overcast, with continual rain and clouds." Starting from the extreme southeast and traveling northwest, one passes the famous white chalk cliffs of Dover which face France, the undulating meadows of Sussex and Kent, the cathedral town of Canterbury, London, and then Oxford. Heading directly north through the center of the island one can see the industrial centers of Birmingham, Manchester, and Leeds, the "dark Satanic mills" that poet William Blake so disliked. Off to the left then, towards the Irish Sea, is the hilly Lake District celebrated by the Romantic poets. To the right, on the North Sea, are the sites of the famous old monasteries, Lindisfarne, Jarrow, Wearmouth, and Whitby, where Christianity flourished in England over a thousand years ago. Directly north over the wall of Hadrian is Macbeth country, Robert Burns country, the mountains lost in cloud, the islands, wild moorlands, and narrow valleys of Scotland. These are geographical facts viewed from the outside, but what England really is and what England really means has been summed up once and for all by a particularly talented native:

> This royal throne of kings, this sceptered isle,
> This earth of majesty, this seat of Mars,
> This other Eden, demi-Paradise;
> This fortress built by Nature for herself
> Against infection and the hand of war;

> This happy breed of men, this little world;
> This precious stone set in the silver sea,
> Which serves it in the office of a wall,
> Or as a moat defensive to a house,
> Against the envy of less happier lands;
> This blessed plot, this earth, this realm, this England.
>
> Shakespeare, *Richard II*

The People

The shores of England were washed by wave after wave of foreign invaders, each adding something to the English character, each absorbed to some extent to form eventually a unified nation. The Celts are the earliest people important to our story. Their migrations to England from the Continent began about eight hundred years before the birth of Christ. The Welsh language and the Gaelic spoken today in parts of Ireland have developed in a direct line from the language spoken by these Celts. One of their tribes, the Brythons, gave Britain its name. Their legends of the young warrior-hero Cuchulainn (ko͞o kul′ in) and of the tragic and beautiful Deirdre are still a living part of English literature.

By the middle of the first century before Christ, the Roman army under Julius Caesar had worked its way through Gaul to the straits of Dover. The first few landings were unsuccessful. It was not until the next century, in 43 A.D., that the Romans established a beachhead in Kent and carried the standards of their legions and the civilization of Rome west and north, driving the ferocious but poorly organized natives ahead of them. Signs of the civilization they brought are still visible: the wall built by Hadrian in the north to keep the Picts in Scotland, an outdoor theater near London, the mineral water baths at the famous Victorian resort Bath, the roads that can still be followed between the major centers of Roman law, commerce, and military life. But after four hundred years, Rome itself was threatened by the migrations of huge tribes across Europe. The distant island no longer seemed important and many of the troops were drawn back to bolster the defenses in Italy. Under constant threat from the Picts in the north, the never fully subdued Celts in the west, and the Anglo-Saxon pirates at sea, the armyless Romans could not long hold out. Prior to 400 A.D. we can not properly speak of an England (Angle land) at all.

From the chaotic years that followed comes the story, mostly legend surrounding an elusive kernel of fact, of King Arthur who was able for a time to unify the Celts and keep off the Anglo-Saxon invaders. But only for a time. By the year 449 the next wave broke on English shores and the Germanic Angles, Saxons, and Jutes made the island their home. This was the beginning of the Anglo-Saxon, or Old English, period. Sussex, Essex, and Wessex were held by the Saxons, while the Angles moved farther north. The Anglo-Saxons brought with them their vigorous life as warriors on the move, their belief in witches, magic, and sacred trees and groves; they brought their gods of darkness, war, and thunder (Tiw, Woden, and Thor), who were to be honored on separate days of the week; and they brought also their belief in Wyrd, the iron unchangeable Fate that rules over all.

The Language

The English language, now spoken by some 275 million people throughout the world, developed directly from the language of the Anglo-Saxon invaders. But its story starts much earlier. We are at the end of a process at least five thousand years old. About the year 3000 B.C. a group of loosely confederated tribes roamed the plains of western Russia north of the Black Sea. They spoke various dialects of a language which scholars have partially reconstructed and labeled Indo-European. As the tribes grew larger they tended to wander apart in search of food and living space. The dialects of those who wandered south developed into Latin and Greek. The Germanic tribes who wandered west gradually evolved the language they spoke when they entered England.

Modern English is basically Anglo-Saxon in origin, but it owes a heavy debt to Latin also. It is surprising, however, to learn that only a handful of Latin words came into our language as a result of some four centuries of Roman occupation of Britain. Some Latin words had already been picked up by the Anglo-Saxons during their contact with Roman border guards in Europe—our modern word *cook,* for example, from the Latin *coquere.* Other words entered the language from the influence of the early missionaries who brought Christianity and education to the British Isles.

A reading of "The Lord's Prayer," printed here in Anglo-Saxon (or Old English, as it is sometimes called), will show you what our language looked like at this stage of its development. The *sound* rather than the *form* of certain Anglo-Saxon characters is reproduced here.

Faeder ūre, thū the eart on heofunum,
Sī thīn nama gehālgod.
Tōbecume thīn rīce.
Gewurthe thīn willa on earthan swā swā on heofunum.
Ure gedaeghwāmlican hlāf syle ūs tō daeg.
And forgyf ūs ūre gyltas,
swā swā wē forgyfath ūrum gyltendum.
And ne gelāed thū ūs on costnunge,
Ac ālys ūs of yfele. Sōthlīce.

The language is still not ours entirely. Old English was a highly *inflected* language; that is, many words changed their form slightly according to their use in the sentence. The tendency over the centuries has been for these inflections to become fewer and fewer. Modern English has almost no inflections except in verbs and pronouns. Modern English, moreover, unlike Old English, is not unilingual.° Ease of communication beyond national boundaries and a liberal attitude toward word borrowing have contributed to the richness and variety of Modern English.

Christianity

A final element and our stage is set. It is an element that plays a dramatic part in the first period of British literature.

We might call it the next wave of invaders to land on British shores and change the character of the land and its people. It was an invasion on two fronts.

Christianity had come to England during the Roman occupation, and was now preserved only by the Celts who had fled before the Anglo-Saxons. England, which had sent missionaries to Ireland earlier, now found itself a missionary territory. The Irish monks, starting from the island of Iona off the west coast of Scotland, evangelized the northern tribes and set up the great centers of learning and civilization at Lindisfarne, Whitby, and Jarrow on the east coast. Meanwhile, another front had opened in the south. The Venerable Bede describes, in his *Ecclesiastical History of the English People*, how Pope Gregory sent St. Augustine[1] at the head of a group of monks to bring the message of Christianity to England; how before they even arrived they were terrified by the thought of "that barbarous, savage, and unbelieving nation whose language they did not even know"; how they received an encouraging letter from Gregory and went on to land in England in 597 and tell the Anglo-Saxons, with amazing success, about heaven and the new life they could lead; how Christianity spread towards the north until it joined with the Irish missionaries working there.

This is the state of England, its language, its people, and its religion, when the story of English literature begins. The history of its literature is usually divided into three major periods, determined by the characteristics of the language used in its production. The Anglo-Saxon (or Old English) period dates from 449, the year the Anglo-Saxon invaders began to overrun England. The Norman invasion in 1066 is taken as the end of the Old English period and the beginning of Middle English. Contact with the French helped develop the language to a point where, with a bit of instruction and practice, a modern speaker of English can recognize Middle English as

[1]Frequently called St. Austin by the British; not to be confused with the more famous bishop and theologian, St. Augustine, who had written his *Confessions* two centuries earlier.

definitely his own language. The next period of change was due to many things: the end of the long, bitter Wars of the Roses; widespread use of the printing press which helped standardize the language and offered a wider audience to writers; the awakening of man's interest, stimulated by explorations, in far-off places and new forms of government; development of scientific methods; and the interest in philosophic speculation and the graceful style of speaking that an educated man could acquire, both of these the result of the new interest in the writings of ancient Greece and Rome. A convenient date for the beginning of this period of Modern English is 1485, the year the Tudors came to the throne of England and also the year that a British printer, William Caxton, published the *Morte d'Arthur* of Sir Thomas Malory, one of the first works of British literature to be printed. Because of the complexities of these five hundred years of Modern English—because literature itself did not stand still—we find many subdivisions within the Modern English period.

The Anglo-Saxon Period

449-1066

Unit One

THE AGE OF HEROES

(OLD ENGLISH)

The subject matter of Old English literature has its roots in the Heroic Age of the Germanic tribes. Their world appears dark and alien to us, a hostile world of famine and warfare, of wild beasts, ruthless climate, and sudden death – all focused around the smoky fire of the mead hall. The social structure of their society was simple: a small ruling nobility who were expected to show leadership, bravery, and generosity and dispense an elementary "eye for an eye and tooth for a tooth" kind of justice, and those who served them with loyalty and subordination in war and peace. At the lowest rung of this class society were slaves who could be bought and sold like cattle. Recollections of this pre-Christian life on the Continent furnish much of the material for their literature. A period of high culture began in England when this stream of tough-minded barbarians from northern Europe met the equally tough-minded Christians from southern Europe and Ireland.

Monks are popularly thought of as people retired from the world and its interests. This concept does not fit the Benedictine monks of the Anglo-Saxon period in England, who were very much a part of their world. Because they believed that culture and the growth of civilization went hand-in-hand with Christianity, they developed magnificent centers of learning from which education spread throughout England and beyond, so that British scholars were known in the ninth and tenth centuries as "the schoolmasters of Europe." Because they believed that to know the people and their hopes and ideals was part of the job of the apostle and the preacher, they developed a truly professional interest in the literature of the Anglo-Saxons.

They searched out and wrote down the stories and songs of these people. What we know of Anglo-Saxon literature, both the tales that were part of their long scopic[1] tradition as well as the newer literature created by a few artistically talented monks, is due to the monastic copyists whose manuscripts we now possess.

The manuscripts which have survived represent, of course, only a small part of what must have been created in the Anglo-Saxon period. Whether what survives is the best, we have no means of knowing. *Beowulf* comes down to us in a single manuscript which is now safe in the British Museum after many damaging adventures. Three other ancient volumes—the *Exeter Book*, the *Vercelli Book*, and the *Junius Manuscript*—contain nearly all the rest of the Old English poetry that we know.

The Ecclesiastical History of the English People

The Venerable Bede (673-735) is one of the outstanding figures of the period. He seems never to have traveled more than a few miles from his monastery at Jarrow, but his mind went out to embrace the whole world of history, music, classical literature, astronomy, and philosophy. His greatest work is *The Ecclesiastical History of the English People*. It is a monument of scholarship, for he tried conscientiously to separate fiction from fact in the chaotic chronicles available to him; it is one of the rare reliable source books for this area of European history.

Bede describes the first contact between these two powerful forces, the Anglo-Saxons who had just conquered England and the Christian message they had never heard before. The selection entitled "The Conversion of King Edwin" tells of the dramatic point in history where these two streams met and began to flow as one.

The Wanderer

"The Wanderer," which is in the *Exeter Book*, is a 115-line lyrical lament in which the purely pagan Anglo-Saxon

[1]SCOPIC—The scops (pronounced skōpz or skəpz) were professional bards equipped with a stock of stories memorized in rhythmic lines and a talent for improvising new stories to celebrate tribal festivals or conquests.

tradition can be isolated rather clearly. It is the lament of a man who, having lost his protecting lord, wanders over the waters to find a resting place. In dreams his vanished happiness returns to him, but day brings only bleakness, desolation, snow, and the sea. The poem was written down under the influence of Christianity, but it reveals the qualities of generosity and loyalty admired by the Anglo-Saxons, the dependence of warrior upon king and companions, and the melancholy sense of hopelessness under the hand of Fate.

The Seafarer

Another poem in the *Exeter Book*, "The Seafarer," is usually presented as a dialogue between an old man, who knows from bitter experience the joyless life of the sea, and a youth, who will not be deterred from leading a sailor's life.

Beowulf

The fusion of Christian and pagan elements is found in the epic *Beowulf*. When the Anglo-Saxons first came to England they had as part of their store of tales the very old legends that had been passed on for centuries and finally had clustered around the name of Beowulf, an actual Swedish warrior who lived during the early sixth century. A Christian poet, some genius whose name has not been preserved for us, reworked this material and incorporated it into a unified poem of 3,182 lines shortly after the year 700. The only surviving copy from Anglo-Saxon times was produced about the year 1000 and narrowly escaped destruction in 1536, when Henry VIII emptied the monasteries, and again in 1731, when it was rescued from the flames that nearly destroyed the collection of Sir Robert Cotton. Modern interest in the poem dates from the first printed edition of the poem in 1815.

Aristotle has defined the *epic* as "an imitation of serious subjects in a grand kind of verse . . . in narrative form . . . based on a single action, one that is a complete whole in itself . . . . The characters celebrated should be of lofty type." The essential story is usually quite simple, and progress is made throughout towards a definite goal. But the path taken is seldom the shortest one. Numerous episodes and "flashbacks" lead to detours. In other words, the epic moves slowly and majestically, developing in detail the characteristics of greatness of its leading man, the epic hero.

There is always one central heroic character who embodies, to some extent, the outstanding characteristics of his race. This hero is often presented as a model of those ideals and virtues which the author feels his present hearers need in order to achieve their national greatness. He is usually involved in a struggle against opposing forces of nature, of men and supermen; it is through his deeds and by his efforts as a representative of his people that the episodes, each one of which is often complete in itself, are linked together and unified in a continuous narrative. As Professor William Paton Ker points out in his *Epic and Romance,* "The grandeur and magnitude of the epic lies not so much in the elevated language, nor in the greatness of theme, nor in the length of the poem as in the greatness of soul of the hero."

There are two types of epic, the folk epic and the literary epic. The folk epic originated among the people, and passed through a long period of telling before it reached its written form. The poet who finally made it a unified poem is usually unknown. The *Iliad* and the *Odyssey* of Homer, which tell of the last days of the Trojan War and the struggle of Ulysses to reach and save his own kingdom of Ithaca, after the fall of Troy, are the finest examples of the folk epic in the literature of the world. *The Nibelungenlied,* the German folk epic, tells the stories of the Germanic characters of the sixth and seventh centuries, Brunhild, Siegfried, and Hagen, later commemorated in the operas of Richard Wagner. *The Song of Roland,* the great epic of France, recounts how Roland, one of Charlemagne's Twelve Peers, died bravely because of the treachery of his own stepfather in betraying the cause of Charlemagne in his fight against the Saracens. *Beowulf* is the only folk epic in the English language.

The literary epic is the conscious product of one known writer. But the poet chooses his materials from respected traditions. To some extent, the literary epic also reflects the thought and opinions of the age in which it was written. The greatest literary epic in the English language is Milton's *Paradise Lost*.

We may briefly summarize the essential elements of the epic as follows:

The plot is a unified story whose direct action is short, but whose implied action is on a sweeping scale. (Virgil tries to shape the whole history of Rome, and Milton to "justify the ways of God to men.") There is one central, heroic character acting in relation both to lesser men and to superhuman forces. The setting is in the distant past, either legendary or supernatural. The mood is noble and dignified, religious and sublime. The literary conventions often include formal introductions (invocations), genealogies to establish the nobility of main characters, catalogues of names and places, and formal speeches written in a lofty style.

Beowulf is one of the oldest epics in any European language. The only other surviving remains of national epic poetry in this period are a 50-line fragment of *Finsburh*, a portion of which appears in *Beowulf*, and two short fragments (63 lines in all) of *Waldere*.

Although the material in *Beowulf* is pagan and Scandinavian in background, there can be no doubt of its Christian spirit. "The epic emerges at last as a Christian poem. This mutation, moreover, is not merely a matter of altered phrases, or of interpolated references to the Christian faith, but is a deeply pervasive infusion of Christian spirit coloring thought and judgment, governing motive and action, a continuous and active agent in the process of transformation."[2] Pagan elements remain, however. For example,

[2]Charles W. Kennedy, *Beowulf: The Oldest English Epic*, Oxford University Press, 1940, xlix.

side by side we find references to the blind power of Wyrd, or Fate, and to the omnipotence and providence of God. But just as often it is implied that Fate is controlled by the Christian God. Again, the origin of Grendel and his dam° from the Scandinavian water troll is lost in the poet's identification of these monsters as the adversaries of God. Reference to the Old Testament runs throughout the poem in unmistakably Christian terms. The portrait of Beowulf is that of a powerful pagan warrior whose best qualities are redeemed and elevated by the power of grace. R. W. Chambers has said: "It is just this which makes the Seventh Century in England so exciting an epoch. Christian gentleness, working upon the passions of the Heroic Age, produces at once a type which is the rough outline of what later becomes the medieval ideal of the knight, or the modern ideal of the gentleman."[3]

The verses of *Beowulf* are characterized by a strong rhythmic beat. But in order to understand the rhythm of this epic, we must broaden somewhat the ideas we have from the rather confining rules of later poetry. Here are the norms that the author of *Beowulf* followed:

1. Each line is broken by a pause in the middle, a *caesura*.
2. There are, usually, two natural word accents in each half-line, no matter how many syllables.
3. The most strongly accented syllable in each half-line begins with the same consonant sound *(alliteration)*.

The following example, lines 185-6 of the present text, will illustrate this pattern.

Tha cóm of *m*óre under *m*íst-hleóthum
Gréndel góngan Gódes yrre báer.
(Then came from the moors, under the misty hollows,
Grendel going, god's wrath he bore.)

The translation you will read skillfully preserves some of these characteristics and will help you imagine the spell of excitement this rhythm created as the scop recited his tale.

[3]"Beowulf and the 'Heroic Age,'" *Man's Unconquerable Mind* (London: Jonathan Cape, 1939), p. 65.

One further characteristic of Old English Poetry is the use of *kennings*—the picturesque linking of nouns as poetic expressions. Thus the body is a "bone-cage," the sea is the "whale-path," and when a man speaks he "unlocks his word-hoard." Several of these kennings are preserved in Charles W. Kennedy's translation.

Caedmon and Cynewulf

Two other poets are worthy of note here, though we know little about them except their names. The first English poet known to us by name is Caedmon, who, according to a passage in Bede, lived till middle age in the monastery at Whitby. Then, in a vision, he was called by name and told to sing of God the Creator. He composed verses and, when he awoke, remembered them and composed others like them. Caedmon turned into song many of the Biblical stories. Cynewulf's name appears after four of the manuscript poems now extant. One of these two poets may have been the author of "The Dream of the Rood," which has been called the most splendid of the Old English religious poems.

King Alfred

No survey of the Old English period would be complete without mentioning the work of King Alfred (849-901). His major political work was subduing the Danish invaders and confining them, by the treaty of Wedmore in 878, to live peaceably in a broad strip of land covering almost one-third of England towards the north. To remedy the widespread illiteracy partly caused by decades of fighting these Vikings or Norsemen, he established a school system which taught the people to read and write English (Anglo-Saxon); Latin was to be a second language offered to advanced students. To encourage the use of English, Alfred himself translated and adapted several books from the original Latin, Augustine's *Soliloquies* and Boethius' *Consolations of Philosophy* among them. He also commissioned the English version of Bede's *Ecclesiastical History,* as well as the *Anglo-Saxon Chronicles,* a work which summarized British history from the first landing of Julius Caesar, and to which a yearly record of events was to be added until almost a century after the Norman invasion. For his own work and for the encouragement he gave to others Alfred has been called by literary historians "The Father of English Prose."

The Conversion of King Edwin

(From *The Ecclesiastical History of the English People,* Book II)

THE VENERABLE BEDE

At this time the nation of the Northumbrians, that is, the nation of the Angles that live on the north side of the river Humber, with their king, Edwin, received the faith through the preaching of Paulinus. This Edwin, as a reward of his receiving the faith, and as an earnest° of his share in the heavenly kingdom, received an increase of that which he enjoyed on earth, for he reduced under his dominion all the borders of Britain that were provinces either of the aforesaid nation, or of the Britons, a thing which no British king had ever done before . . . .

For some time he delayed to receive the word of God at the preaching of Paulinus, and used to sit several hours alone, and seriously to ponder with himself what he was to do, and what religion he was to follow. Then the man of God came to him, laid his right hand on his head, and asked whether he knew that sign. The king, in a trembling condition, was ready to fall down at his feet, but he raised him up, and in a familiar manner said to him, "Behold, by the help of God you have escaped the hands of the enemies whom you feared. Behold, you have of His gift obtained the kingdom which you desired. Take heed not to delay that which you promised to perform; embrace the faith, and keep the precepts of Him who, delivering you from temporal° adversity,° has raised you to the honor of a temporal kingdom; and if, from this time forward, you shall be obedient to His will, which through me He signifies to you, He will not only deliver you from the everlasting torments of the wicked, but also make you partaker with Him of His eternal kingdom in Heaven."

The king, hearing these words, answered that he was both willing and bound to receive the faith which he taught; but that he would confer about it with his principal friends and counselors, to the end that if they also were of his opinion, they might all together be cleansed in Christ the Fountain of Life. Paulinus consenting, the king did as he said; for, holding a council with the wise men, he asked of every one in particular what he thought of the new doctrine, and the new worship that was preached. To which the chief of his own priests, Coifi, immediately answered, "O king, consider what this is which is now preached to us; for I verily declare to you, that the religion which we have hitherto professed has, as far as I can learn, no virtue in it. For none of your people has applied himself more diligently to the worship of our gods than I; and yet there are many who receive greater favors from you, and are more preferred than I, and are more prosperous in all their undertakings. Now if the gods were good for any thing, they would rather forward me, who have been more careful to serve them. It remains, therefore, that if upon examination you find those new doctrines, which are now preached to us, better and more efficacious, we immediately receive them without delay."

Another of the king's chief men, approving of his words and exhortations, presently added: "The present life of man, O king, seems to me, in comparison to that time which is unknown to us, like to the swift flight of a sparrow through the room wherein you sit at supper in winter, with your commanders and ministers, and a good fire in the midst, whilst the storms of rain and snow prevail abroad; the sparrow, flying in at one door, and immediately out at another, whilst he is within, is safe from the wintry storm; but after a short space of fair weather, he immediately vanishes out of your sight, into the dark winter from which he had emerged. So this life of man appears for a short space, but of what went before, or what is to follow, we are utterly ignorant. If, therefore, this new doctrine contains something more certain, it seems justly to deserve to be followed." The other elders and king's counselors, by Divine inspiration, spoke to the same effect . . . .

King Edwin, therefore, with all the nobility of the nation, and a large number of the common sort, received the faith, and the washing of regeneration, in the eleventh year of his reign, which is the year of the incarnation of our Lord 627, and about one hundred and eighty after the coming of the English into Britain . . . .

Consult the Dictionary of Questions and do especially Questions 13, 25, 44, 45, 57, 133, and 145.

The Wanderer

Translated by Charles W. Kennedy

Oft to the Wanderer, weary of exile,
Cometh God's pity, compassionate love,
Though woefully toiling on wintry seas
With churning oar in the icy wave,
Homeless and helpless he fled from Fate.
Thus saith the Wanderer mindful of misery,
Grievous disasters, and death of kin:
"Oft when the day broke, oft at the dawning,
Lonely and wretched I wailed my woe.
No man is living, no comrade left,
To whom I dare fully unlock my heart.
I have learned truly the mark of a man
Is keeping his counsel and locking his lips,
Let him think what he will! For, woe of heart
Withstandeth not Fate; a failing spirit
Earneth no help. Men eager for honor

Bury their sorrow deep in the breast.
So have I also, often, in wretchedness
Fettered my feelings, far from my kin,
Homeless and hapless, since days of old,
When the dark earth covered my dear lord's face,
And I sailed away with sorrowful heart,
Over wintry seas, seeking a gold-lord,
If far or near lived one to befriend me
With gift in the mead-hall and comfort for grief.
Who bears it, knows what a bitter companion,
Shoulder to shoulder, sorrow can be,
When friends are no more. His fortune is exile,
Not gifts of fine gold; a heart that is frozen,
Earth's winsomeness° dead. And he dreams of the
hallmen,[1]
The dealing of treasure, the days of his youth,
When his lord bade welcome to wassail° and feast.
But gone is that gladness, and never again
Shall come the loved counsel of comrade and king.
Even in slumber his sorrow assaileth,
And, dreaming, he claspeth his dear lord again,
Head on knee, hand on knee, loyally laying,
Pledging his liege as in days long past.
Then from his slumber he starts lonely-hearted,
Beholding gray stretches of tossing sea,
Sea-birds bathing, with wings outspread,
While hail-storms darken, and driving snow.
Bitterer then is the bane of his wretchedness,
The longing for loved one: his grief is renewed.
The forms of his kinsmen take shape in the silence;[2]
In rapture he greets them; in gladness he scans
Old comrades remembered. But they melt into air
With no word of greeting to gladden his heart.
Then again surges his sorrow upon him;
And grimly he spurs on his weary soul
Once more to the toil of the tossing sea.
No wonder therefore, in all the world,

[1]Companions serving the same leader.
[2]The Wanderer begins to dream here.

If a shadow darkens upon my spirit
When I reflect on the fates of men—
How one by one proud warriors vanish
From the halls that knew them, and day by day
All this earth ages and droops unto death.
No man may know wisdom till many a winter
Has been his portion. A wise man is patient,
Not swift to anger, nor hasty of speech,
Neither too weak, nor too reckless, in war,
Neither fearful nor fain,[3] nor too wishful of wealth,
Nor too eager in vow—ere he know the event.
A brave man must bide when he speaketh his boast
Until he know surely the goal of his spirit.
A wise man will ponder how dread is that doom
When all this world's wealth shall be scattered and
  waste—
As now, over all, through the regions of earth,
Walls stand rime-covered[4] and swept by the winds.
The battlements crumble, the wine-halls decay;
Joyless and silent the heroes are sleeping
Where the proud host fell by the wall they defended.
Some battle launched on their long, last journey;
One a bird bore o'er the billowing sea;
One the gray wolf slew; one a grieving earl
Sadly gave to the grave's embrace.
The Warden of men[5] hath wasted this world
Till the sound of music and revel is stilled,
And these giant-built structures stand empty of life.
He who shall muse on these mouldering ruins,
And deeply ponder this darkling° life,
Must brood on old legends of battle and bloodshed,
And heavy the mood that troubles his heart:
'Where now is the warrior? Where is the war-horse?
Bestowal of treasure, and sharing of feast?
Alas! the bright ale-cup, the byrny-clad[6] warrior,

[3]Eager.
[4]Frost-covered.
[5]God.
[6]Wearing armor.

The prince in his splendor—those days are long sped
In the night of the past, as if they never had been!'
And now remains only, for warriors' memorial,
A wall wondrous high with serpent shapes carved.
Storms of ash-spears have smitten the earls,
Carnage of weapon, and conquering Fate.
Storms now batter these ramparts of stone;
Blowing snow and the blast of winter
Enfold the earth; night-shadows fall
Darkly lowering,° from the north driving
Raging hail in wrath upon men.
Wretchedness fills the realm of earth,
And Fate's decrees transform the world.
Here wealth is fleeting, friends are fleeting,
Man is fleeting, maid is fleeting;
All the foundation of earth shall fail!"
Thus spake the sage in solitude pondering.
Good man is he who guardeth his faith.
He must never too quickly unburden his breast
Of its sorrow, but eagerly strive for redress.°
And happy the man who seeketh for mercy
From his heavenly Father, our fortress and strength.

Do especially Questions 14, 34, 41, 44, 63, 133, and 135. Consult the Model Poem on page 61.

The Seafarer

Translated by LaMotte Iddings

PART I

I can sing of myself a true song, of my voyages telling,
How oft through laborious days, through the wearisome
hours

I have suffered; have borne tribulations; explored in my ship,
Mid the terrible rolling of waves, habitations of sorrow.
Benumbed by the cold, oft the comfortless night-watch hath held me
At the prow of my craft as it tossed about under the cliffs.
My feet were imprisoned with frost, were fettered with ice-chains,
Yet hotly were wailing the querulous° sighs round my heart;
And hunger within me, sea-wearied, made havoc of courage.
This he, whose lot happily chances on land, doth not know;
Nor how I on the ice-cold sea passed the winter in exile,
In wretchedness, robbed of my kinsmen, with icicles hung.
The hail flew in showers about me; and there I heard only
The roar of the sea, ice-cold waves, and the song of the swan;
For pastime the gannets'° cry served me; the kittiwakes'° chatter
For laughter of men; and for mead-drink the call of the sea-mews.
When storms on the rocky cliffs beat, then the terns, icy-feathered,
Made answer; full oft the sea-eagle forebodingly screamed,
The eagle with pinions wave-wet. There none of my kinsmen
Might gladden my desolate soul; of this little he knows
Who possesses the pleasures of life, who has felt in the city
Some hardship, some trifling adversity, proud and wine flushed.
How weary, I oft had to tarry upon the sea-way!

The shadows of night became darker, it snowed from the north;
The world was enchained by the frost; hail fell upon earth;
'Twas the coldest of grain. Yet the thoughts of my heart now are throbbing
To test the high streams, the salt waves in tumultuous play.
Desire in my heart ever urges my spirit to wander
To seek out the home of the stranger in lands afar off.
There is no one that dwells upon earth, so exalted in mind,
So large in his bounty, nor yet of such vigorous youth,
Nor so daring in deeds, nor to whom his liege lord is so kind,
But that he has always a longing, a seafaring passion
For what the Lord God shall bestow, be it honor or death.
No heart for the harp has he, nor for acceptance of treasure,
No pleasure has he in a wife, no delight in the world,
Nor in aught save the roll of the billows; but always a longing,
A yearning uneasiness, hastens him on to the sea.
The woodlands are captured by blossoms, the hamlets grow fair,
Broad meadows are beautiful, earth again bursts into life,
And all stir the heart of the wanderer eager to journey,
So he meditates going afar on the pathway of tides.
The cuckoo, moreover, gives warning with sorrowful note,
Summer's harbinger sings, and forebodes to the heart bitter sorrow.
The nobleman comprehends not, the luxurious man,
What some must endure, who travel the farthest in exile.
Now my spirit uneasily turns in the heart's narrow chamber,
Now wanders forth over the tide, o'er the home of the whale,

To the ends of the earth—and comes back to me. Eager and greedy,
The lone wanderer screams, and resistlessly drives my soul onward,
Over the whale-path, over the tracts of the sea.

PART II

The delights of the Lord are far dearer to me than this dead,
Fleeting life upon earth, for I can not believe that earth's riches
For ever endure. Each one of three things, ere its time comes,
Is always uncertain: violence, age, and disease
Wrench the soul away, doomed to depart. This is praise from the living,
From those who speak afterwards, this the best fame after death—
That ere he departed he labored, and wrought daring deeds
'Gainst the malice of fiends, and the devil; so men shall extol him,
His praise among angels shall live, ever, world without end,
His the blessing of life everlasting, and joy mid the hosts.
The days have departed, all pomps of earth's kingdom have vanished;
There now are no kings, no emperors now, no gold-givers
As of yore, when they wrought in their midst the most glorious deeds,
And lived in the lordliest power. This glory has fallen,
Delights have all vanished away; the weak ones remain,
And these govern the world, obtaining their pleasure with effort.
Power has declined, earth's glory grows aged and sear,
Like every man now in the world; old age overtakes him,

His countenance loses its color, gray-haired he laments;
He has seen his old friends, sons of princes, consigned°
to the earth.
This garment of flesh has no power, when the spirit
escapes,
To drink in the sweet nor to taste of the bitter; it then
Has no power to stretch forth the hands or to think with
the mind.
Though the grave should be covered with gold by the
nearest of kin,
Be buried along with the dead in masses of treasure,
Still that will not go with them. Gold can no substitute
be
For the fear of the Lord, to the soul which is laden with
sin,
Which aforetime, so long as it lived, kept that treasure
concealed.
Great is the fear of the Lord; the earth trembles
before it;
He established the unmovable earth, the world and the
heavens.
Foolish is he who stands not in awe of the Lord—
Unexpectedly death comes upon him; but happy is he
Who lives humble in mind, to him cometh honor from
heaven;
God doth establish the soul that believes in His
might.
One should check a strong will, and should govern it
firmly,
Be true unto men, and be clean in his manner of life . . . .
Fate, God the Creator, is stronger than any man's will.
Come, let us reflect where our home is, consider the
way
By which we go thither; then let us each strive to press
forward
To joy everlasting, where life has its source in God's
love,
Where is heavenly hope. Then to Him who is holy be
thanks,

Because He hath honored us; thanks to the Ruler of
Heaven,
The Lord everlasting, throughout all the ages! Amen.

Do especially Questions 14, 32, 34, 44, 47, 63, 146, and 157. Consult the Model Poem on page 61.

Beowulf

Translated by Charles W. Kennedy

[*The poet introduces Hrothgar, king of the Danes, by a description of his famous ancestors and their accomplishments. The glory of his rule was symbolized in the great hall which he built and called Heorot*[1] *or Hall of the Hart.*[2] *But in time disaster came to the land in the form of two monsters: Grendel and his mother, both of hideous shape and superhuman size.*]

To Hrothgar was granted glory in war,
Success in battle; retainers bold
Obeyed him gladly; his band increased
To a mighty host. Then his mind was moved
To have men fashion a high-built hall,
A mightier mead-hall than man had known,
Wherein to portion to old and young
All goodly treasure that God had given,
Save only the folk-land, and lives of men.
His word was published to many a people
Far and wide o'er the ways of the earth
To rear a folk-stead richly adorned;

[1] Pronounced hā'ō rot.
[2] Deer

The task was speeded, the time soon came
That the famous mead-hall was finished and done.
To distant nations its name was known,
The Hall of the Hart; and the king kept well
His pledge and promise to deal out gifts,
Rings at the banquet. The great hall rose
High and horn-gabled, holding its place
Till the battle-surge of consuming flame
Should swallow it up. . . .
Then an evil spirit who dwelt in the darkness
Endured it ill that he heard each day
The din of revelry ring through the hall,
The sound of the harp, and the scop's sweet song.
A skillful bard sang the ancient story
Of man's creation; how the Maker wrought
The shining earth with its circling waters;
In splendor established the sun and moon
As lights to illumine the land of men;
Fairly adorning the fields of earth
With leaves and branches; creating life
In every creature that breathes and moves.
So the lordly warriors lived in gladness,
At ease and happy, till a fiend from hell
Began a series of savage crimes.
They called him Grendel, a demon grim
Haunting the fen-lands,[3] holding the moors,
Ranging the wastes, where the wretched wight[4]
Made his lair with the monster kin;
He bore the curse of the seed of Cain
Whereby God punished the grievous guilt
Of Abel's murder. Nor ever had Cain
Cause to boast of that deed of blood;
God banished him far from the fields of men;
Of his blood was begotten an evil brood,
Marauding monsters and menacing trolls,[5]

[3]Marshes.
[4]A creature, a living being, from the Anglo-Saxon.
[5]A troll is a preternatural being, celebrated in Scandinavian folklore. It is sometimes referred to as a dwarf, sometimes as a giant, living in caves, hills, or the sea.

Goblins and giants who battled with God
A long time. Grimly He gave them reward!

[*Night raids by Grendel gradually diminished the number of Hrothgar's warriors and turned the hall into a place of fear and dread. For twelve years this terror lay upon the land.*

But news of this dire calamity which was afflicting the Danes reached the land of the Geats in southern Sweden, where it came to the knowledge of the hero Beowulf. Against the advice of his uncle, Hygelac, and eager for fame and adventure, Beowulf with a small band of followers sailed for Denmark to match his strength against Grendel.]

Then tales of the terrible deeds of Grendel
Reached Hygelac's thane° in his home with the Geats;
Of living strong men he was the strongest,
Fearless and gallant and great of heart.
He gave command for a goodly vessel
Fitted and furnished; he fain would sail
Over the swan-road to seek the king
Who suffered so sorely for need of men.
And his bold retainers found little to blame
In his daring venture, dear though he was;
They viewed the omens, and urged him on.
Brave was the band he had gathered about him,
Fourteen stalwarts° seasoned and bold,
Seeking the shore where the ship lay waiting,
A sea-skilled mariner sighting the landmarks.
Came the hour of boarding; the boat was riding
The waves of the harbor under the hill.
The eager mariners mounted the prow;
Billows were breaking, sea against sand.
In the ship's hold snugly they stowed their trappings,
Gleaming armor and battle-gear;
Launched the vessel, the well-braced bark,
Seaward bound on a joyous journey.
Over breaking billows, with bellying sail
And foamy beak, like a flying bird

The ship sped on, till the next day's sun
Showed sea-cliffs shining, towering hills
And stretching headlands. The sea was crossed,
The voyage ended, the vessel moored.
And the Weder people waded ashore
With clatter of trappings and coats of mail;
Gave thanks to God that His grace had granted
Sea-paths safe for their ocean-journey.

[*Beowulf and his company landed and were challenged by the Danish coast guard, who noted the princely form and bearing of Beowulf. After learning his name and his mission, the coast guard led the company over the stone-paved streets where the Hall of the Hart gleamed in its glory. They piled their war-gear and boar-crested helmets outside the hall. A warrior bore the news of their coming to Hrothgar. Beowulf entered proudly.*]

Then the bold one rose with his band around him,
A splendid massing of mighty thanes;
A few stood guard as the Geat gave bidding
Over the weapons stacked by the wall.
They followed in haste on the heels of their leader
Under Heorot's roof. Full ready and bold
The helmeted warrior strode to the hearth;
Beowulf spoke; his byrny[6] glittered,
His war-net woven by cunning of smith:
"Hail! King Hrothgar! I am Hygelac's thane,
Hygelac's kinsman. Many a deed
Of honor and daring I've done in my youth.
This business of Grendel was brought to my ears
On my native soil. The sea-farers say
This best of buildings, this boasted hall,
Stands dark and deserted when sun is set,
When darkening shadows gather with dusk.
The best of my people, prudent and brave,
Urged me, King Hrothgar, to seek you out;

[6]A coat of mail.

They had in remembrance my courage and might.
Many had seen me come safe from the conflict,
Bloody from battle; five foes I bound
Of the giant kindred, and crushed their clan.
Hard-driven in danger and darkness of night
I slew the nicors[7] that swam the sea,
Avenged the woe they had caused the Weders,
And ended their evil—they needed the lesson!
And now with Grendel, the fearful fiend,
Single-handed I'll settle the strife!
Prince of the Danes protector of Scyldings,
Lord of nations, and leader of men,
I beg one favor—refuse me not,
Since I come thus faring from far-off lands—
That I may alone with my loyal earls,
With this hardy company, cleanse Hart-Hall.
I have heard that the demon in proud disdain
Spurns all weapons; and I too scorn—
May Hygelac's heart have joy of the deed—
To bear my sword, or sheltering shield,
Or yellow buckler, to battle the fiend.
With hand-grip only I'll grapple with Grendel;
Foe against foe I'll fight to the death,
And the one who is taken must trust to God's grace!"

[*Hrothgar gratefully welcomed Beowulf amid royal entertainment and entrusted to Beowulf and his band the task of freeing Heorot from the scourge of Grendel. At the height of the celebration the jealous and proud Danish courtier, Unferth, alluded to a swimming match between Beowulf and Breca in which Unferth claimed that Breca had bested Beowulf. Unferth predicted an evil fate for Beowulf if he dared to encounter Grendel. But Beowulf replied:*]

"My good friend Unferth, addled with beer,
Much have you made of the deeds of Breca!
I count it true that I had more courage,

[7] Water monsters.

More strength in swimming than any other man.
In our youth we boasted—we were both of us boys—
We would risk our lives in the raging sea.
And we made it good! We gripped in our hands
Naked swords, as we swam in the waves,
Guarding us well from the whales' assault.
In the breaking seas he could not outstrip me,
Nor would I leave him. For five nights long
Side by side we strove in the waters
Till racing combers° wrenched us apart,
Freezing squalls, and the falling night,
And a bitter north wind's icy blast.
Rough were the waves; the wrath of the sea-fish
Was fiercely roused; but my firm-linked byrny,
The gold-adorned corselet that covered my breast,
Gave firm defense from the clutching foe.
Down to the bottom a savage sea-beast
Fiercely dragged me and held me fast
In a deadly grip; nonetheless it was granted me
To pierce the monster with a point of steel.
Death swept it away with the swing of my sword.
  The grisly sea-beasts again and again
Beset me sore; but I served them home
With my faithful blade as was well-befitting.
Bloody with wounds, at the break of day,
They lay on the sea-beach slain with the sword.
No more would they cumber the mariner's course
On the ocean deep. From the east came the sun,
Bright beacon of God, and the seas subsided;
I beheld the headlands, the windy walls.
Fate often delivers an undoomed earl
If his spirit be gallant! And so I was granted
To slay with the sword-edge nine of the nicors.
I have never heard tell of more terrible strife
Under dome of heaven in darkness of night,
Nor of man harder pressed on the paths of ocean.
But I freed my life from the grip of the foe
Though spent with the struggle. The billows bore me,
The swirling currents and surging seas,

To the land of the Finns. And little I've heard
Of any such valiant adventures from you!
Neither Breca nor you in the press of battle
Ever showed such daring with dripping swords—
Though I boast not of it! But you stained your blade
With blood of your brothers, your closest of kin;
And for that you'll endure damnation in hell,
Sharp as you are! I say for a truth,
Son of Ecglaf, never had Grendel
Wrought such havoc and woe in the hall,
That horrid demon so harried your king,
If your heart were as brave as you'd have men think!
But Grendel has found that he never need fear
Revenge from your people, or valiant attack
From the Victor-Scyldings;[8] he takes his toll,
Sparing none of the Danish stock.
But soon will I show him the stuff of the Geats,
Their courage in battle and strength in the strife."

[*Hrothgar's hopes were high as he listened to Beowulf's bold resolve. At nightfall, Beowulf and his men took over the hall, sleeping with their weapons at hand. Then suddenly out of the mist and darkness, Grendel burst in upon them.*]

From the stretching moors, from the misty hollows,
Grendel came creeping, accursed of God,
A murderous ravager minded to snare
Spoils of heroes in high-built hall.
Under clouded heavens he held his way
Till there rose before him the high-roofed house,
Wine-hall of warriors gleaming with gold....
Storming the building he burst the portal,
Though fastened of iron, with fiendish strength;
Forced open the entrance in savage fury
And rushed in rage o'er the shining floor.
A baleful glare from his eyes was gleaming
Most like to a flame. He found in the hall
Many a warrior sealed in slumber,

[8] Pronounced shil' dingz; descendants of Scyld. The Danes.

A host of kinsmen. His heart rejoiced;
The savage monster was minded to sever
Lives from bodies ere break of day,
To feast his fill of the flesh of men.
But he was not fated to glut his greed
With more of mankind when the night was ended!
The hardy kinsman of Hygelac waited
To see how the monster would make his attack.
The demon delayed not, but quickly clutched
A sleeping thane in his swift assault,
Tore him to pieces, bit through the bones,
Gulped the blood and gobbled the flesh,
Greedily gorged on the lifeless corpse,
The hands and the feet. Then the fiend stepped nearer,
Sprang on the Sea-Geat lying out-stretched,
Clasping him close with his monstrous claw.
But Beowulf grappled and gripped him hard,
Struggled up on his elbow; the shepherd of sins
Soon found that never before had he felt
In any man other in all the earth
A mightier hand-grip; his mood was humbled,
His courage fled; but he found no escape!
He was fain to be gone; he would flee to the darkness,
The fellowship of devils. Far different his fate
From that which befell him in former days!
The hardy hero, Hygelac's kinsman,
Remembered the boast he had made at the banquet;
He sprang to his feet, clutched Grendel fast,
Though fingers were cracking, the fiend pulled free.
The earl pressed after; the monster was minded
To win his freedom and flee to the fens.
He knew that his fingers were fast in the grip
Of a savage foe. Sorry the venture,
The raid that the ravager made on the hall.
There was din in Heorot. For all the Danes,
The city-dwellers, the stalwart Scyldings,
That was a bitter spilling of beer!
The walls resounded, the fight was fierce,
Savage the strife as the warriors struggled.

The wonder was that the lofty wine-hall
Withstood the struggle, nor crashed to earth
The house so fair; it was firmly fastened
Within and without with iron bands
Cunningly smithied; though men have said
That many a mead-bench gleaming with gold
Sprang from its sill as the warriors strove.
The Scylding wise men had never weened
That any ravage could wreck the building
Till the time when the swelter and surge of fire
Should swallow it up in a swirl of flame.
  Continuous tumult filled the hall;
A terror fell on the Danish folk
As they heard through the wall the horrible wailing,
The groans of Grendel, the foe of God
Howling his hideous hymn of pain,
The hell-thane shrieking in sore defeat.
He was fast in the grip of the man who was greatest
Of mortal men in the strength of his might,
Who would never rest while the wretch was living,
Counting his life-days a menace to man.
  Many an earl of Beowulf brandished
His ancient iron to guard his lord,
To shelter safely the peerless prince.
They had no knowledge, those daring thanes,
When they drew their weapons to hack and hew,
To thrust to the heart, that the sharpest sword,
The choicest iron in all the world,
Could work no harm to the hideous foe.
On every sword he had laid a spell,
On every blade; but a bitter death
Was to be his fate; far was the journey
The monster made to the home of fiends.
  Then he who had wrought such wrong to men,
With grim delight as he warred with God,
Soon found that his strength was feeble and failing
In the crushing hold of Hygelac's thane.
Each loathed the other while life should last!
There Grendel suffered a grievous hurt,

A wound in the shoulder, gaping and wide;
Sinews snapped and bone-joints broke,
And Beowulf gained the glory of battle.
Grendel, fated, fled to the fens,
To his joyless dwelling, sick unto death.
He knew in his heart that his hours were numbered,
His days at an end. For all the Danes
Their wish was fulfilled in the fall of Grendel.
The lord of the Geats made good to the East-Danes
The boast he had uttered; he ended their ill.
The token was clear when the bold in battle
Laid down the shoulder and dripping claw—
Grendel's arm—in the gabled hall!

[*With morning came joy as the Danes gathered in the Hall to view the huge claw of Grendel. They traced the bloody steps of the monster to the edge of the dark pool. As they returned from the fen to Heorot, with horses proudly prancing, a minstrel sang a song in praise of Beowulf. A great feast was prepared at which Hrothgar honored Beowulf and his men with many gifts in the banquet hall. Hour after hour the revelry continued.*

But the coming of night brought new horror in the person of Grendel's mother, who came to avenge her son's death. She entered among the sleeping Danish thanes, woke them to struggle, and carried off Aeschere, the beloved comrade of Hrothgar. The Danes were filled with despair. In the morning, the aged Hrothgar speedily summoned Beowulf, who had no knowledge of the new attack.]

The hero came tramping into the hall
With his chosen band—the boards resounded—
Greeted the leader, the Ingwine[9] lord,
And asked if the night had been peaceful and pleasant.
  Hrothgar spoke, the lord of the Scyldings:
"Ask not of pleasure; pain is renewed
For the Danish people. Aeschere is dead!

[9] Pronounced ing′ wi nə; Danish.

He was my comrade, closest of counsellors,
My shoulder-companion as side by side
We fought for our lives in the welter of war,
As an earl should be, a prince without peer,
Such was Aeschere, slain in the hall
By the wandering demon! I know not whither
She fled to shelter, proud of her spoil,
Gorged to the full . . . .

Oft in the hall I have heard my people,
Comrades and counsellors, telling a tale
Of evil spirits their eyes have sighted,
Two mighty marauders who haunt the moors.
One shape, as clearly as men could see,
Seemed woman's likeness, and one seemed man,
An outcast wretch of another world,
And huger far than human form.
Grendel my countrymen called him, not knowing
What monster-brood spawned him, what sire begot.
Wild and lonely the land they live in,
Wind-swept ridges and wolf-retreats,
Dread tracts of fen where the falling torrent
Downward dips into gloom and shadow
Under the dusk of the darkening cliff.
Not far in miles lies the lonely mere°
Where trees firm-rooted and hung with frost
Overshroud the wave with shadowing gloom.
And there a portent° appears each night,
A flame in the water; no man so wise
Who knows the bounds of its bottomless depth.
The heather-stepper, the horned stag,
The antlered hart hard driven by hounds,
Invading that forest in flight from afar
Will turn at bay and die on the brink
Ere ever he'll plunge in that haunted pool.
'Tis an eerie spot! Its tossing spray
Mounts dark to heaven when high winds stir
The driving storm, and the sky is murky,

And with foul weather the heavens weep.
On your arm only rests all our hope!
Not yet have you tempted those terrible reaches,
The region that shelters that sinful wight.
Go if you dare! I will give requital
With ancient treasure and twisted gold.
As I formerly gave in guerdon[10] of battle,
If out of that combat you come alive."
  Beowulf spoke, the son of Ecgtheow:[11]
"Sorrow not, brave one! Better for man
To avenge a friend than much to mourn.
All men must die; let him who may
Win glory ere death. That guerdon is best
For a noble man when his name survives him.
Then let us rise up, O ward of the realm,
And haste us forth to behold the track
Of Grendel's dam."

[*Hrothgar leaped up and thanked God for the hero's words. Then the Danes and the Geats journeyed together over the moorlands to the watery depths. Beowulf girded himself with his war-gear and Unferth gave him his sword, Hrunting. Beowulf accepted the sword and asked that all his treasure be sent to Hygelac if he died in the combat.*]

After these words the prince of the Weders
Awaited no answer, but turned to the task,
Straightway plunged in the swirling pool.
Nigh unto a day he endured the depths
Ere he first had view of the vast sea-bottom.
Soon she found, who had haunted the flood,
A ravening hag, for a hundred half-years,
Greedy and grim, that a man was groping
In daring search through the sea-troll's home.
Swift she grappled and grasped the warrior
With horrid grip, but could work no harm,
No hurt to his body; the ring-locked byrny

[10]Pronounced gûr′ dən; a reward.
[11]Pronounced ej′ the ō̄; the father of Beowulf.

Cloaked his life from her clutching claw;
Nor could she tear through the tempered mail
With her savage fingers. The she-wolf bore
The ring-prince down through the watery depths
To her den at the bottom; nor could Beowulf draw
His blade for battle, though brave his mood.
Many a sea-beast, strange sea-monsters,
Tasked him hard with their menacing tusks,
Broke his byrny and smote him sore.
Then he found himself in a fearsome hall
Where water came not to work him hurt,
But the flood was stayed by the sheltering roof.
There in the glow of the firelight gleaming
The hero had view of the huge sea-troll.
He swung his war-sword with all his strength,
Withheld not the blow, and the savage blade
Sang on her head its hymn of hate.
But the bold one found that the battle-flasher
Would bite no longer, nor harm her life.
The sword-edge failed at his sorest need.
But fixed of purpose and firm of mood
Hygelac's earl was mindful of honor;
In wrath, undaunted, he dashed to earth
The jewelled sword with its scrolled design,
The blade of steel; staked all on strength,
On the might of his hand, as a man must do
Who thinks to win in the welter of battle
Enduring glory; he fears not death.

[*Beowulf gripped the shoulder of Grendel's dam and hurled her to the ground. In the tussle, she staggered Beowulf, knelt upon him and drew her dagger, but the steel of his corselet shielded his breast. Swiftly he sprang to his feet, seized a heavy sword from her war-gear, and struck with fury.*]

Thrust at the throat, broke through the bone-rings;
The stout blade stabbed through her fated flesh.
She sank in death; the sword was bloody;

The hero joyed in the work of his hand.
The gleaming radiance shimmered and shone
As the candle of heaven shines clear from the sky.

[*The Danes who had watched at the edge of the pool believed Beowulf had been killed when they saw the water suddenly stained with blood. In despair they returned to Heorot. But the loyal Geats waited until at last Beowulf swam up from the depths bearing Grendel's head and the hilt of the sword whose blade had melted. Joyfully his companions accompanied him to the Hall of the Hart. Here again Hrothgar celebrated with an elaborate feast and giving of gifts. When all were silent Hrothgar praised the young hero who had been strong and loyal, and bade young Beowulf to strive for virtue, as the ancient Danish King Heremod did not.*]

"Strive for virtue! I speak for your good.
'Tis a wondrous marvel how mighty God
In gracious spirit bestows on men
The gift of wisdom, and goodly lands,
And princely power! He rules over all!
He suffers a man of lordly line
To set his heart on his own desires,
Awards him fullness of worldly joy,
A fair home-land, and the sway of cities,
The wide dominion of many a realm,
An ample kingdom, till, cursed with folly,
The thoughts of his heart take no heed of his end.
He lives in luxury, knowing not want,
Knowing no shadow of sickness or age;
No haunting sorrow darkens his spirit,
No hatred or discord deepens to war;
The world is sweet to his every desire,
And evil assails not—until in his heart
Pride overpowering gathers and grows.
Then is his heart pierced, under his helm,
His soul in his bosom, with bitter dart.
He has no defense for the fierce assaults

Of the loathsome Fiend. What he long has cherished
Seems all too little! In anger and greed
He gives no guerdon of plated rings.
Since God has granted him glory and wealth
He forgets the future, unmindful of Fate.
But it comes to pass in the day appointed
His feeble body withers and fails;
Death descends, and another seizes
His hoarded riches and rashly spends
The princely treasure, imprudent of heart.
Beloved Beowulf, best of warriors,
Avoid such evil and seek the good,
The heavenly wisdom. Beware of pride!"

[*With the morning light Beowulf came to take his leave. He returned Hrunting with thanks to Unferth, and with his companions triumphantly took sail for home.*]

The ship was launched.
Cleaving the combers of open sea
They dropped the shoreline of Denmark astern.
A stretching sea-cloth, a bellying sail,
Was bent on the mast; there was groaning of timbers;
A gale was blowing; the boat drove on.
The foamy-necked plunger plowed through the billows,
The ring-stemmed ship through the breaking seas,
Till at last they sighted the sea-cliffs of Geatland,
The well-known headlands; and, whipped by the wind,
The boat drove shoreward and beached on the sand.

[*Upon their arrival in the land of the Geats, they were royally welcomed and feasted by Hygelac and his court. Beowulf recounted his wonderful adventures and shared with Hygelac and the queen the gifts which Hrothgar had given him. Hygelac, in turn, gave Beowulf a gift of a costly sword, and a stately hall with a large estate. So ends the first section of the narrative.*

Years went by and at last Beowulf ruled the kingdom of the Geats. During his old age a fire dragon ravaged his land after one of his men stole a golden flagon° from a huge treasure which the dragon had guarded for three hundred years. With fire and flame the dragon burned dwellings and filled all hearts with terror. Beowulf prepared for battle against this menace to his people. Armed with his sword, Naegling, and an iron shield, the king, with eleven comrades, was guided by the thief to the dragon's fen.]

The thirteenth man in the hurrying throng
Was the sorrowful captive who caused the feud.

[*Standing near the stone entrance from which hot steam poured forth, Beowulf and the dragon entered into mortal combat. His sword, Naegling, broke. All of his companions turned and fled into the forest to save their lives except the youthful Wiglaf.*]

He saw his king
Under his helmet smitten with heat.
He thought of the gifts which his lord had given,
The wealth and the land of the Waegmunding[12] line
And all the folk-rights his father had owned;
Wiglaf spoke in sorrow of soul,
With bitter reproach rebuking his comrades:
"I remember the time, as we drank in the mead-hall,
When we swore to our lord who bestowed these rings
That we would repay for the war-gear and armor,
The hard swords and helmets, if need like this
Should ever befall him.
Now is the day that our lord has need
Of the strength and the courage of stalwart men.
Let us haste to succor his sore distress
In the horrible heat and merciless flame.
God knows I had rather the fire should enfold
My body and limbs with my gold-friend and lord."

[12]Pronounced wag′ mun ding; the family to which Wiglaf and Beowulf belonged.

[*Finally the dragon fastened his fangs in Beowulf's throat and the hero suffered a deadly wound. Wiglaf thrust his sword into the dragon's body and Beowulf with dying strength cut the beast in two with his dagger. Now dying Beowulf spoke:*]

"My armor and sword I would leave to my son
Had Fate but granted, born of my body,
An heir to follow me after I'm gone.
For fifty winters I've ruled this realm,
And never a lord of a neighboring land
Dared strike with terror or seek with sword.
In my life I abode by the lot assigned,
Kept well what was mine, courted no quarrels,
Swore no false oaths. And now for all this
Though my hurt is grievous, my heart is glad.
When life leaves body, the Lord of mankind
Cannot lay to my charge the killing of kinsmen!"

[*Beowulf asked Wiglaf to gaze on the gold of the dragon's loot. Wiglaf returned to his dying lord with heaps of the treasure. As he looked upon the spoils, Beowulf gave thanks to God who gave the grace to win these riches for his people. He spoke again to young Wiglaf:*]

"Heed well the wants, the need of my people;
My hour is come, and my end is near.
Bid warriors build, when they burn my body,
A stately barrow[13] on the headland's height.
It shall be for remembrance among my people
As it towers high on the Cape of the Whale,
And sailors shall know it as Beowulf's Barrow,
Sea-faring mariners driving their ships
Through fogs of ocean from far countries."
Then the great-hearted king unclasped from his throat
A collar of gold, and gave to his thane;

[13]A grave covered by an earthen mound.

Gave the young hero his gold-decked helmet,
His ring and his byrny, and wished him well.
"You are the last of the Waegmunding line.
All my kinsmen, earls in their glory,
Fate has sent to their final doom,
And I must follow." These words were the last
The old king spoke ere the pyre received him,
The leaping flames of the funeral blaze,
And his breath went forth from his bosom, his soul
Went forth from the flesh, to the joys of the just.

[*The cowardly thanes crept back and looked at Wiglaf as he sat by the king's body. Wiglaf again upbraided them and told of the contempt with which the cowardly deed would be spoken of in future years. A messenger rode along the cliffs relating the sad news to Beowulf's people and prophesying the fall of the nation. The body of the dead dragon was tumbled over the cliff into the sea. In accordance with Beowulf's dying wish, a funeral pyre was built on the headland and a barrow constructed in which was buried the dragon's treasure. The funeral pyre was kindled, and round the pyre wound the mourning warriors as they proclaimed his virtue and fame.*]

They sang their dirge and spoke of the hero
Vaunting his valor and venturous deeds.
So is it proper a man should praise
His friendly lord with a loving heart,
When his soul must forth from the fleeting flesh.
So the folk of the Geats, the friends of his hearth,
Bemoaned the fall of their mighty lord;
Said he was kindest of worldly kings,
Mildest, most gentle, most eager for fame.

Do especially Questions 11, 15, 17, 20, 57, 63, 65, 75, 83, 86, 88, 89, 97, 102, 105, 109, 111, 142, 148, and 157. Consult the Model Poem on page 61.

PROBLEM QUESTIONS

1. It has been said that *Beowulf* is a work of pagan literature, tampered with by some later monkish copyist who interpolated lines here and there, obviously breaking the flow of the narrative and giving the poem a veneer of Christian piety. Discuss, supporting your statements with references from the text.

2. What evidence is there that the author of *Beowulf* may have intended his hero to stand as a model for the ideal Anglo-Saxon leader? Cite items in the poem that support this statement. In what respects could Beowulf serve as a model for leaders in our own society?

3. What evidence is there that Beowulf's foes are symbols, meant to represent abstract qualities or forces rather than simple literal monsters?

4. "The Wanderer" and "The Seafarer" tell us a great deal about the lives, the temperament, and the ideals of the Anglo-Saxons. Support this statement with specific references to both poems.

The Medieval Period

1066-1485

Unit Two

THE AGE OF CHIVALRY

(MIDDLE ENGLISH)

The scholars who chose the term "Middle English" made a particularly fortunate choice. The language written then shows strongly its Anglo-Saxon roots and yet is quite close to the modern English that was to evolve from it. But even more significantly, the greatest author of the period, Geoffrey Chaucer, stands roughly midway, chronologically, between the composition of *Beowulf* and the works of literature which are being produced in our own day.

The Norman invasion of England under William the Conqueror (1066) is a matter of political rather than literary history, though the date is a convenient one to use. It marks a high point of French intellectual and cultural leadership in Europe. The French influence would have been felt in England, to some extent at least, even if there had been no conquest. The vigorous Norsemen, who had moved into northern France and taken over the land, the language, and the religion of the country, now set the styles in education, architecture, and literature. Edward the Confessor, who had ruled in England from 1042 until 1066, had been educated in Normandy by the people who finally took over his kingdom. Stout castles, part of the London Tower, and the cathedrals of Durham and Ely still stand as fine examples of Norman architecture.

With the Norman invasion, the Anglo-Saxon language went underground. Norman rulers and churchmen supplanted the native nobility and hierarchy. French was spoken and written by the educated and aristocratic, and for over two centuries English was identified with the rustic and uneducated. By the first half of the thirteenth century the aristocracy had lost their holdings on the French mainland, and the tendency was to look upon England as a permanent home. The Hundred Years War (1338-1453) was a series of attempts to regain their claims, but it helped rather to solidify the feeling that England was the object of loyalty and patriotism against the injustice of the French. England had absorbed still another wave of invaders.

The English that reappears about 1300 is a changed language. The cumbersome grammar has been simplified; the word endings have dropped or changed to an often silent *e*, and the vocabulary has been immensely enriched by permanent borrowings from the French. From the French come most of the Latin root words in our language, concepts of "curtesye" and "gentillesse," and most of the literary forms and conventions of the period. A sample of the East Midland dialect, spoken in and around London, is given at the beginning of the Chaucer selections. This dialect, one of five major dialects (Kentish, Southern, East Midland, West Midland, and Northern) significantly different from each other, eventually emerged as "standard" English. The four literary forms treated here were heavily influenced by French writers.

The Lyric

Originally, the *lyric* was a short poem set to music. It was a new form, one not found among our Old English sources. Scholars have found its predecessors in the hymns of the early Church and in the *chansons* of the wandering troubadours of France. The famous Harleian Manuscript, compiled about 1320, contains some of the best lyrics, but many have been preserved only by accident: the scribe would scribble a few lines in the margin to start a new pen, or fill out a page of expensive parchment with a few stanzas. Most of the English lyrics are simply reworkings of conventional themes: the purity of the Virgin Mary, the joy of spring, unrequited love, melancholy about the transience of life. The British lyric frequently triumphs over the conventional theme by the brilliant originality with which it is handled. The freshness and beauty of these poems is apparent even though the musical notation has, in most cases, not survived.

A new type of prosody was introduced by the French poets: accents came regularly every second or third syllable, and rhyme held the poem in a tighter unity. The following lines illustrate this pattern, and show also that alliteration was not completely forgotten.

Lenten[1] is come with love to towne
With blosmen[2] and with birddes roune.[3]

A new voice is heard in British poetry: a lyric lightness expressed by new poetic techniques.

The great bulk of Middle English lyrics is religious or moral. Few secular lyrics have been preserved. "The Cuckoo Song" is the oldest of the lyrics. The music is still extant and shows that it is a *round* meant to be sung by six voices. Perhaps the long English winter, with its sickness, hunger, and inactivity, accounts for the poet's joyful reaction to spring.

The Popular Ballad

The popular ballad is essentially a narrative song preserved orally among unsophisticated people fairly homogeneous in environment and outlook. Only a handful of those we now possess were written down before 1600. Scholars in the eighteenth and nineteenth centuries collected them from old manuscripts and from country people who still sang them, and experimented with techniques for finding out what the earliest versions really were. But it is the nature of oral literature to change, to be improved or ruined by later authors depending on one's point of view. Where did the ballads come from? The Brothers Grimm, of fairy tale fame, held the theory that "folk" ballads (not the "literary" ones whose authors are known) were produced by a whole community as a form of recreation. This idea has been abandoned or modified by later scholars. Sir Arthur Quiller-Couch finds

[1]Spring.
[2]Blossoms.
[3]Song.

indications that many of the best ballads were composed about the same time, probably within a rather small area; he suggests that there was one "man of genius who gave these songs their immortal impress and taught it to others." Many have resisted his theory. The problem of ballad authorship remains.

The *ballad stanza*, which will occur frequently in later English literature, contains four iambic lines alternating tetrameter and trimeter, with an *a b c b* rhyme scheme. Characteristic of the ballad is the grim realism and hint of treachery in "The Twa Corbies"; the slow unveiling of action and motive in "Edward, Edward"; the remnant of some actual event behind "Sir Patrick Spens"; the "incremental repetition" of "The Wife of Usher's Well." Among the most familiar themes of the English and Scottish popular ballads of this period we find the supernatural, unrequited love, border warfare, religion, and the Robin Hood cycle. Although the tragic note predominates, there are a number of humorous ballads; these center chiefly around the battle of the sexes. Ballads were intended to be sung, and, as the name implies, were connected at some time with dancing.

The Metrical Romance

The *metrical romance* was a popular form of medieval entertainment, comparable to the novel in present-day literature. As a literary form it was imported from France. The subject matter was always romantic love, chivalry, and religious idealism; the purpose was usually didactic.° The characters—knights, ladies, evil magicians—engaged in spectacular episodes amid gorgeously described scenes of court and forest. The stories were drawn from the legends of Charlemagne and his fights with the Moors; from ancient legends of Achilles, Aeneas, and Caesar; or from the Celtic legends of King Arthur and the Knights of the Round Table.

Sir Gawain and the Green Knight is generally considered to be the finest of the medieval romances. All that is known about the author is that he wrote about 1320, that he lived about one hundred and fifty miles northwest of London (he wrote in a difficult Midland dialect), that he has been called the Pearl Poet (one of the other three poems in the only surviving manuscript of *Gawain* is called "The Pearl"), and that he was far superior to the ordinary medieval romancer. In spite of the influence of French meter, the Pearl Poet was part of the alliterative revival of the fourteenth century; some of the alliteration is preserved in the present translation. However, the influence of French prosody is not lacking. The 2,530 lines of the poem are divided into stanzas of unequal length, each terminated by a "bob-in-wheel": a line of monometer (bob) is followed by four lines of trimeter. The five lines are rhymed *a b a b a*.

One indication of the skill of the Pearl Poet is his spendthrift use of conventional themes. A lesser author would have used only one or a few tales from his store and would have linked them together in an episodic manner, each tale usually having a strong moral at the end. The Pearl Poet was able to weave several conventional elements into one unified work of art: the challenge to the court, the exchange of blows, the beheaded knight, the elaborate hunting scenes, the triple temptation, and the exchange of winnings. The hero of a run-of-the-mill romance is a two-dimensional character whose inner life is not described as Gawain's is. The purpose of most medieval literature was didactic, and *Gawain and the Green Knight* is no exception. The Pearl Poet wished to recall faded ideals of chivalry, courtesy, chastity. But since his artistry embodies this purpose, there is no need for him to say at the end, "the moral of the story is . . . ." He leaves that to be worked out by his intelligent audience.

The Metrical Tale

The greatest author of medieval England is Geoffrey Chaucer and his outstanding work is *The Canterbury Tales*. One of his earliest critics was the poet John Dryden, who said that Chaucer "has taken into the compass of his *Canterbury Tales* the various manners and humors (as we now call them) of the whole English nation in his age. Not a single character has escaped him.... Some of his persons are vicious, and some virtuous; some are unlearned, or (as Chaucer calls them) lewd, and some are learned.... There is such a variety of game springing up before me that I am distracted in my choice, and know not which to follow. 'Tis sufficient to say, according to the proverb, that here is God's plenty."

The Canterbury Tales is a framework piece. Some thirty people are described as traveling from London to visit the shrine of the martyred St. Thomas à Becket at Canterbury. The Host suggests that, in order to make the trip more pleasant, each pilgrim tell two stories on the way to Canterbury and two on the way back. The work consists of only twenty-four tales, several of them unfinished. The stories are connected by means of the pervading personality of the Host, who gives a unity to the entire work. Most of these stories are not only interesting in themselves but also appropriate to the teller. The details which we have learned from the brilliant and colorful thumbnail sketches of the "Prologue" and from the conversational "links" between the tales are developed and deepened by the stories the characters tell.

Chaucer is first in the line of great English satirists. He appears aloof and detached, a simple observer, but his descriptions cut through to the foibles and affectations of the Prioress, to the worldliness of the Monk who made up his own rules as he went along, to the smugness and complacency of the worldly guildsmen. But Chaucer was not an "Angry Young Man." His humor could delight in the zest of the embroidered young Squire and the hearty vulgarity of the Wife of Bath. And his sympathy was won by the gentlemanly Knight and the poor scholarly Clerk.

Chaucer's pilgrims present an exciting pageant of medieval life, and the stories cover nearly the whole ground of medieval poetry. Most of the types (romance, bestiary,° fabliau,° and hagiology,° to name a few) are represented in *The Canterbury Tales*. One of the best known of Chaucer's tales is the bestiary of Chanticleer and Dame Partlet. The story included in this volume is the Clerk's tale of the patient Griselda.

William Langland

William Langland, whose work is not represented in this book, was a contemporary of Chaucer and the Pearl Poet, but entirely different from either of them. He was a restless man who burned with pity and indignation at the evils of his time. He wrote his thoughts and dreams into his poem, *The Vision of Piers Plowman.* With a sharp and angry pen he cried out against social injustice, challenged both churchmen and the wealthy to reform, and stingingly satirized the unworthy clergy, monks, and friars. Langland wanted to reconstruct and revitalize society with a new spiritual vigor. *Piers Plowman* is like a rough pageant of his century, in which we brush shoulders with the common man as he wears the smell of the streets on his tattered clothing. We hear the laughter and cries of the poor as they act and talk, sometimes raucously and rowdily, sometimes gravely and profoundly.

Everyman

The early Church was responsible for the disappearance of Roman drama towards the decline of the Empire. The paganism and obscenity of these later Roman spectacles could not be tolerated by Christian officials. There is irony, then, in the fact that when European drama reappeared several centuries later, it had developed directly from the liturgical services of the Church. Part of the liturgy of the Church involved reading, at the beginning of the service, a short piece of appropriate scripture which was followed by the antiphonal recitation of a psalm (introit). This antiphonal singing—one half of the choir answering the other—developed into "dialogue" with characters taking different parts. The earliest of these dialogues (called *tropes*) centered around the visit of the women to Christ's tomb. Other incidents in the life of Christ offered opportunity for more detailed development once the idea caught on. The Visit of the Magi and the Slaughter of the Innocents provided an opportunity for pantomime. The next step was to costume people as various Old Testament prophets and have them speak their own words of the Messiah who was to come. Dramatizations of some of the Old Testament heroes, such as Noah, provided humor as well as excitement for these audiences. One can easily imagine the strain these developments put upon the traditional order of the liturgy; it is also easy to imagine how popular these short playlets were with the people. It worked out to everyone's satisfaction when guilds took over their production and presented them in the public square with more and more details added each year.

There are three types of medieval drama: Mystery, Miracle, and Morality plays. Mystery plays are mainly concerned with the saving events recorded in the Bible; they developed directly from the process described above. Several towns, particularly in the north of England, had large repertories or cycles of such plays, dramatizing everything from the Creation to Doomsday. We still possess manuscripts of two of the best cycles, York and Wakefield. Along with these Mystery plays, and not always easily distinguishable from them, are the Miracle plays, concerned mainly with apocryphal tales about Mary or miraculous events in the lives of the saints.

Everyman is the finest example of the third category, the Morality play. It is a later development and quite different from the other two types. The Morality play is characterized by its personification of abstract qualities (Gluttony, Strength, Kinship, and others) and by its use of general classes as individual characters (Everyman, Good Deeds, and so forth). The plays are allegorical and didactic; they are concerned with such basic human issues as death, salvation, and damnation. The perennial vitality of *Everyman* has been proven over and over again in recent years by highly successful college and professional productions.

The End of the Middle Ages

Sir Thomas Malory's *Morte d'Arthur* stands as a fitting symbol for the end of one era and the beginning of another, though the year of its publication, 1485, must not be considered as a single year of abrupt and dramatic transition from medieval to modern. Malory's story is a long look backward, recapitulating much of medieval literature. In 1137 Geoffrey of Monmouth's Latin history of the British kings had given the first sizable collection of Arthur stories. Layamon's *Brut* retold the stories in English about the year 1205. From there the French took up the legend and added many new characters and incidents. The material reappears in English in the many romances referred to earlier. Little is known about Sir Thomas Malory, except that he was usually somewhat on the other side of the law. During one of his stays in prison he completed his long reorganization of the many Arthur sources available to him.

The publication of the *Morte d'Arthur* looks forward, too, to a new era for Western civilization. It was one of the first works of British literature to be popularized by the printing press, a recent invention that had been brought into England a few years before by William Caxton. Little knowing what interest the book would have for centuries to come, Caxton felt it necessary to write an edifying preface to such antique material: "To the intent that noble men may see and learn the noble acts of chivalry, the gentle and virtuous deeds that some knights used in those days, by which they came to honor, and how they that were vicious were punished and oft put to shame and rebuke, humbly beseeching all noble lords and ladies that shall see and read in this said book and work, that they take the good and honest acts in their remembrance and follow the same."

The Cuckoo Song

Sumer is icumen in,
Lhude sing cuccu!
Groweth sed and bloweth med[1]
And springth the wode[2] nu.[3]
Sing cuccu!

Awe bleteth after lomb,
Lhouth[4] after calve cu,[5]
Bulluc sterteth, bucke verteth.[6]
Murie[7] sing cuccu!
Cuccu, cuccu,
Wel singes thu, cuccu.
Ne swik[8] thu naver nu!

Sing cuccu nu, Sing cuccu!
Sing cuccu, Sing cuccu nu!

[1]The meadow blossoms.
[2]Wood.
[3]Now.
[4]Loweth.
[5]Cow.
[6]Leaps.
[7]Merrily.
[8]Cease.

Do especially Questions 12, 45, 49, 52, 58, 65, 133, and 148. *Consult the Model Poem on page 61.*

The Twa Corbies

As I was walking all alane,
I heard twa corbies[1] making a mane.[2]
The tane[3] unto the t'other say,
"Where sall we gang and dine today?"

[1]Two crows.
[2]Moan.
[3]One.

"In behint yon auld fail dyke[4]
I wot there lies a new-slain knight;
And naebody kens that he lies there,
But his hawk, his hound, and lady fair."

"His hound is to the hunting gane,
His hawk to fetch the wild-fowl hame,
His lady's ta'en another mate,
So we may mak our dinner sweet."

"Ye'll sit on his white hause-bane[5]
And I'll pick out his bonny blue een;[6]
Wi ae lock o' his gowden hair
We'll theek[7] our nest when it grows bare."

"Mony a one for him makes mane,
But nane sall ken where he is gane;
O'er his white banes, when they are bare,
The wind sall blaw for evermair."

[4]Old turf wall.
[5]Neck-bone.
[6]Eyes.
[7]Thatch.

Do especially Questions 12, 35, 57, 70, 75, 90, and 144. Consult the Model Poem on page 61.

Edward, Edward

"Why dois your brand[1] sae drap wi bluid,
  Edward, Edward?
Why dois your brand sae drap wi bluid,
  And why sae sad gang[2] yee O?"

[1]Sword.
[2]Go.

"Edward, Edward" from *English and Scottish Popular Ballads,* edited by Sargent & Kittredge, Houghton Mifflin Company, Publishers.

"O I hae killed my hauke sae guid,
  Mither, mither,
O I hae killed my hauke sae guid,
  And I had nae mair bot hee O."

"Your haukis bluid was nevir sae reid,
  Edward, Edward,
Your haukis bluid was nevir sae reid,
  My deir son I tell thee O."
"O I hae killed my reid-roan steid,
  Mither, mither,
O I hae killed my reid-roan steid,
  That erst was sae fair and frie[3] O."

"Your steid was auld, and ye hae gat mair,
  Edward, Edward,
Your steid was auld, and ye hae gat mair,
  Sum other dule ye drie[4] O."
"O I hae killed my fadir deir,
  Mither, mither,
O I hae killed my fadir deir,
  Alas, and wae is mee O!"

"And whatten penance wul ye drie for that,
  Edward, Edward?
And whatten penance wul ye drie for that?
  My deir son, now tell me O."
"Ile set my feit in yonder boat,
  Mither, mither,
Ile set my feit in yonder boat,
  And Ile fare ovir the sea O."

"And what wul ye doe wi your towirs and your ha,[5]
  Edward, Edward?
And what wul ye doe wi your towirs and your ha,
  That were sae fair to see O?"

[3]That once was so fair and spirited.
[4]DULE . . . DRIE – Grief . . . suffer, undergo.
[5]Hall.

"Ile let thame stand tul they doun fa,
Mither, mither,
Ile let thame stand tul they doun fa,
For here nevir mair maun I bee O."

"And what wul ye leive to your bairns[6] and your wife,
Edward, Edward?
And what wul ye leive to your bairns and your wife,
Whan ye gang ovir the sea O?"
"The warld is room, late them beg thrae life,
Mither, mither,
The warld is room, late them beg thrae life,
For thame nevir mair wul I see O."

"And what wul ye leive to your ain mither deir,
Edward, Edward?
And what wul ye leive to your ain mither deir?
My deir son, now tell me O."
"The curse of hell frae me sall ye beir,
Mither, mither,
The curse of hell frae me sall ye beir,
Sic counseils ye gave to me O."

[6]Children.

Do especially Questions 12, 15, 35, 41, 58, 70, 73, 84, 90, 93, 94, and 144. Consult the Model Poem on page 61.

Sir Patrick Spens

The king sits in Dumferling toune,
Drinking the blude-reid wine:
"O whar will I get guid sailor,
To sail this schip of mine?"

"Sir Patrick Spens" from *English and Scottish Popular Ballads*, edited by Sargent & Kittredge, Houghton Mifflin Company, Publishers.

Up and spak an eldern knicht,[1]
Sat at the kings richt kne:
"Sir Patrick Spens is the best sailor
That sails upon the se."

The king has written a braid letter,[2]
And signed it wi his hand,
And sent it to Sir Patrick Spens,
Was walking on the sand.

The first line that Sir Patrick red,
A loud lauch[3] lauched he;
The next line that Sir Patrick red,
The teir blinded his ee.[4]

"O wha is this has don this deid,
This ill deid don to me,
To send me out this time o' the yeir,
To sail upon the se!

"Mak haste, mak haste, my mirry men all,
Our guid schip sails the morne."
"O say na sae, my master deir,
For I feir a deadlie storme.

"Late late yestreen I saw the new moone,
Wi the auld moone in hir arme,[5]
And I feir, I feir, my deir master,
That we will cum to harme."

O our Scots nobles wer richt laith[6]
To wet their cork-heild schoone;[7]

[1]An older knight.
[2]A long letter.
[3]Laugh.
[4]Eye.
[5]It is still a superstition among sailors that when the dark part of the moon can be seen inside the horn of the new moon, a storm will follow.
[6]Right loath, very unwilling.
[7]Shoes.

Bot lang owre[8] a' the play wer played,
  Thair hats they swam aboone.[9]

O lang, lang may their ladies sit,
  Wi thair fans into their hand,
Or eir they se Sir Patrick Spens
  Cum sailing to the land.

O lang, lang may the ladies stand,
  Wi thair gold kems[10] in their hair,
Waiting for thair ain deir lords,
  For they'll se thame na mair.

Haf owre, haf owre to Aberdour,[11]
  It's fiftie fadom deip,
And thair lies guid Sir Patrick Spens,
  Wi the Scots lords at his feit.

[8]Long before.
[9]Above.
[10]Combs.
[11]Half over, half over to Aberdour (a small town near Edinburgh).

Do especially Questions 12, 15, 17, 35, 41, 58, 70, 74, 84, 90, and 144. Consult the following Model Poem.

MODEL POEM

Sir Patrick Spens approached from the Seven Views of the *Dictionary of Questions*

FIRST VIEW

1. What is my first impression of the work as a total unit? My first impression is that the author of this ballad has compressed a good story into a very short space. I have the impression that a less skillful author might have expanded here and there and added all kinds of irrelevant details. I find the first reading rather difficult because of the old-fashioned spelling; but this helps to remind me how old the poem actually is, and how much language develops over the centuries.

SECOND VIEW

2. Under which type would I classify the work from a first reading? The poem is a ballad. I notice that "ballad" comes under the larger classification of Narrative Poetry. In my analysis I will have to keep my eyes open to narrative techniques used by the author.

THIRD VIEW

11. What is the theme of the work? The theme seems to be that a man may sometimes encounter suffering as he carries out his duty; but it is the kind of suffering that ennobles a man rather than the kind that degrades or destroys him as a person. Sir Patrick Spens's story seems to come close to tragedy.

FOURTH VIEW

33. Record any noticeable shift from one physical or mental viewpoint to another. I notice that the poem begins by focusing on the king and his court. At the end of stanza 3 the scene shifts directly to Sir Patrick. The last four stanzas move away from the characters for the author's commentary on the story. Thus, the story seems to be divided into three almost equal parts.

41. If the work is *fictional prose* or *narrative poetry*, can I divide the material to indicate the growth and release of tension according to the graph? Even though the story is told briefly, it still shows the classical structure that most stories follow. The king's first question serves as Exposition and sets the story in motion. A note of Complication enters the story when we learn of Sir Patrick's mixed feelings toward the command. He seems to fear the dangers of the trip. The Climax is somewhat muted because it is reported to us indirectly by the narrator: "Thair hats they swam aboone." The Conclusion is also subdued: the ladies quietly waiting as if frozen in a picture, and the Scottish lords fifty fathoms under water.

42. What are the various . . . tragic forces? Sir Patrick feels that there has been foul play. Someone has done him an "ill deid" to have him sent to sea at this time of year. His statement comes in the middle of the poem, but it makes us look back to the beginning where the king is drinking "blude-reid wine" with his courtiers. Is there some intrigue? Does the "eldern knicht" have some reason for wanting Sir Patrick out of the way? Do the ladies at the end of the poem fit into the intrigue at all? The balladeer suggests much more than he actually tells us.

FIFTH VIEW

57. How does the author's use of figurative language and symbols affect the development of the theme? The "*blude*-reid wine" was probably chosen consciously by the author to help establish the mood of tragedy and intrigue. The most striking image, however, appears in lines 25-6, almost the exact center of the poem: the new moon with the old moon in her arms. The fact that it is difficult, at first, to visualize makes it stand out. It is also an image filled with warning of the tragedy to come, as the sailor tells us. The author seems to use such a striking and meaningful image at this central point of the poem to help organize and focus his theme.

66. How does the metrical pattern of the poem help shape the meaning of a particular passage or the total meaning of the poem? "Sir Patrick Spens" is written in the standard ballad meter. This is quite a rigid form, allowing for few variations. Yet nowhere does the language seem forced into a preconceived mold. The form he has chosen for his story allows it to be set to music and sung. I must recall that the tune selected, the sound of the lute or guitar, and the singer's voice would all add another dimension to the enjoyment of the poem.

101. How are the characters integrated with the theme? There is not much room in a poem of this size for elaborate conversation and characterization. Each item must be selected with care. Sir Patrick, for example, is given only a few lines of dialogue, but these seem to characterize him as intelligent and sensitive to the possible dangers of the trip, yet devotedly loyal to his king. Sir Patrick's character is further enhanced by contrast with others around him. All that we are told about the king seems to indicate that he is a heavy drinker surrounded by court intrigue. The ladies at the end of the poem seem colorless and perhaps a bit frivolous with their fans and combs. The contrast adds to the stature of Sir Patrick.

SIXTH VIEW

144. How does the knowledge of the history of literature and the other arts contribute to my understanding of the work? Perhaps my initial prejudice against the quaint spelling in the poem should be modified. I realize on reflection that the printing press was one of the greatest forces for standardizing the language and its spelling. "Sir Patrick Spens" was probably written shortly before the printing press was invented. I can find some value too in this old-fashioned phonetic spelling: it gives me some idea of how our English language was pronounced several hundred years ago.

SEVENTH VIEW

157. How does the present work, as I understand it, compare with other works I have read? There is some similarity in theme between *Beowulf* and "Sir Patrick Spens." Both concern the deeds of heroic men of action. More importantly, both are concerned with a code of absolute loyalty to one's leader. This code, I have come to see, is one of the major themes of early British literature. I would find it hard to compare *Beowulf* and "Sir Patrick Spens." Perhaps it is best to say that one is a very good epic, the other a very good ballad. They have different purposes and different methods, and affect the reader much too differently to be judged finally by the same norms.

The Wife of Usher's Well

There lived a wife at Usher's Well,
  And a wealthy wife was she;
She had three stout and stalwart sons,
  And sent them oer the sea.

They hadna been a week from her,
  A week but barely ane,
Whan word came to the carline[1] wife
  That her three sons were gane.

They hadna been a week from her,
  A week but barely three,
Whan word came to the carline wife
  That her sons she'd never see.

"I wish the wind may never cease,
  Nor fashes[2] in the flood,
Till my three sons come hame to me,
  In earthly flesh and blood."

It fell about the Martinmass,
  When nights are lang and mirk,
The carline wife's three sons came hame,
  And their hats were o the birk.[3]

[1]Old.
[2]Troubles.
[3]Birch-wood.

It neither grew in syke[4] nor ditch
Nor yet in ony sheugh;[5]
But at the gates o Paradise,
That birk grew fair eneugh.

"Blow up the fire, my maidens,
Bring water from the well;
For a' my house shall feast this night,
Since my three sons are well."

And she has made to them a bed,
She's made it large and wide,
And she's taen her mantle her about,
Sat down at the bed-side.

Up then crew the red, red cock,
And up and crew the gray;
The eldest to the youngest said,
" 'T is time we were away."

The cock he hadna crawd but once,
And clapped his wings at a',
When the youngest to the eldest said,
"Brother, we must awa.

"The cock doth craw, the day doth daw,
The channerin[6] worm doth chide;
Gin we be mist out o our place,
A sair pain we maun[7] bide;

"Fare ye weel, my mother dear!
Fareweel to barn and byre![8]
And fare ye weel, the bonny lass
That kindles my mother's fire!"

[4]Trench.
[5]Furrow.
[6]Devouring.
[7]SAIR . . . MAUN—Sore . . . must.
[8]Cow shed.

Do especially Questions 35, 41, 58, 70, 75, 90, and 144. Consult the Model Poem on page 61.

Get Up and Bar the Door

It fell about the Martinmas[1] time,
And a gay time it was then,
When our good wife got puddings to make,
And she's boild them in the pan.

The wind sae cauld blew south and north,
And blew into the floor;
Quoth our goodman[2] to our goodwife,
"Gae out and bar the door."

"My hand is in my hussyfskap,[3]
Goodman, as ye may see;
An it should nae be barrd this hundred year,
It's no be barrd for me."[4]

They made a paction[5] tween them twa,
They made it firm and sure,
That the first word whaeer should speak,
Should rise and bar the door.

Then there came two gentlemen,
A twelve o clock at night,
And they could see neither house nor hall,
Nor coal nor candle-light.

"Now whether is this a rich man's house,
Or whether is it a poor?"
But neer a word wad ane o them speak,
For barring of the door.

[1]Feast of St. Martin, November 11.
[2]Husband.
[3]Housework.
[4]By me.
[5]Pact, agreement.

"Get Up and Bar the Door" from *English and Scottish Popular Ballads,* edited by Sargent & Kittredge, Houghton Mifflin Company, Publishers.

And first they ate the white puddings
  And then they ate the black;
Tho muckle[6] thought the goodwife to hersel,
  Yet neer a word she spake.

Then said the one unto the other,
  "Here, man, tak ye my knife;
Do ye tak off the auld man's beard,
  And I'll kiss the goodwife."

"But there's nae water in the house,
  And what shall we do than?"
"What ails ye at the pudding-broo,[7]
  That boils into the pan?"

O up then started our goodman,
  An angry man was he:
"Will ye kiss my wife before my een,
  And scad[8] me wi' pudding-bree?"

Then up and started our goodwife,
  Gied three skips on the floor:
"Goodman, you've spoken the foremost word,
  Get up and bar the door."

[6]Much.
[7]What's the matter with the pudding broth . . .?
[8]Scald.

Do especially Questions 71, 74, 75, and 90. Consult the Model Poem on page 61.

Barbara Allen's Cruelty

In Scarlet towne, where I was borne,
  There was a faire maid dwellin,
Made every youth crye, "Wel-awaye!"
  Her name was Barbara Allen.

"Barbara Allen's Cruelty" from *Reliques of Ancient English Poetry* by Thomas Percy.

All in the merrye month of May,
When greene buds they were swellin,
Yong Jemmye Grove on his death-bed lay,
For love of Barbara Allen.

He sent his man unto her then,
To the towne where shee was dwellin;
"You must come to my master deare,
Giff[1] your name be Barbara Allen.

For death is printed on his face,
And ore his hart is stealin:
Then haste away to comfort him,
O lovelye Barbara Allen."

Though death be printed on his face,
And ore his harte is stealin,
Yet little better shall he bee
For bonny Barbara Allen.

So slowly, slowly, she came up,
And slowly she came nye him;
And all she sayd, when there she came,
"Yong man, I think y'are dying."

He turned his face unto her strait,
With deadlye sorrow sighing;
"O lovely maid, come pity mee,
Ime on my death-bed lying."

"If on your death-bed you doe lye,
What needs the tale you are tellin;
I cannot keep you from your death;
Farewell," sayd Barbara Allen.

He turned his face unto the wall,
As deadlye pangs he fell in:

[1] If.

"Adieu! adieu! adieu to you all,
Adieu to Barbara Allen."

As she was walking ore the fields,
She heard the bell a knellin;
And every stroke did seem to say,
"Unworthy Barbara Allen."

She turnd her bodye round about,
And spied the corps a coming:
"Laye down, laye down the corps," she said
"That I may look upon him."

With scornful eye she looked down,
Her cheeke with laughter swellin:
Whilst all her friends cryd out amaine:[2]
"Unworthye Barbara Allen."

When he was dead, and laid in grave,
Her harte was struck with sorrowe,
"O mother, mother, make my bed,
For I shall dye to-morrowe.

Hard-harted creature him to slight,
Who loved me so dearlye:
O that I had beene more kind to him,
When he was alive and neare me!"

She, on her death-bed as she laye,
Beg'd to be buried by him;
And sore repented of the daye,
That she did ere denye him.

"Farewell," she sayd, "ye virgins all,
And shun the fault I fell in:
Henceforth take warning by the fall
Of cruel Barbara Allen."

[2]Quickly; loudly.

Do especially Questions 16, 17, 34, 45, 66, 75, and 84. Consult the Model Poem on page 61.

Sir Gawain and the Green Knight

Translated by Theodore Howard Banks, Jr.

I

[The poem opens with mention of the founding of Britain by Felix Brutus. But of all the British kings, Arthur was the most celebrated, "whose renown was next to the Savior's." It was at the court of Camelot where Arthur was celebrating the Christmas festival with his "peerless lords" that the strangest of marvels occurred. Arthur, Queen Guinevere, Sir Gawain[1] *and others are gathered at the high table. An elaborate meal is spread before them, but Arthur will not eat until all are served and some marvelous tale is told; or until some stranger knight seeks permission to joust with one of his court. His desire is soon granted.]*

And scarcely the music had ceased for a moment,
The first course been suitably served in the court,
When a being most dreadful burst through the hall-door,
Among the most mighty of men in his measure.
From his throat to his thighs so thick were his sinews,
His loins and his limbs so large and so long,
That I hold him half-giant, the hugest of men,
And the handsomest, too, in his height, upon horseback.
Though stalwart in breast and in back was his body,
His waist and his belly were worthily small;
Fashioned fairly he was in his form, and in features
Cut clean.
Men wondered at the hue
That in his face was seen.
A splendid man to view
He came, entirely green.

[1]Pronounced gä' win; according to the Arthurian legend, Gawain was the son of Lot, a Scottish king, and Arthur's half-sister, Anna.

All green was the man, and green were his garments:
A coat, straight and close, that clung to his sides,
A bright mantle on top of this, trimmed on the inside
With closely-cut fur, right fair, that showed clearly,
The lining with white fur most lovely, and hood too,
Caught back from his locks, and laid on his shoulders,
Neat stockings that clung to his calves, tightly stretched,
Of the same green, and under them spurs of gold shining
Brightly on bands of fine silk, richly barred;
And under his legs, where he rides, guards of leather.
His vesture was verily color of verdure:[2]
Both bars of his belt and other stones, beautiful,
Richly arranged in his splendid array
On himself and his saddle, on silken designs.
'T would be truly too hard to tell half the trifles
Embroidered about it with birds and with flies
In gay, verdant green with gold in the middle;
The bit-studs, the crupper,[3] the breast-trappings' pendants,
And everything metal enamelled in emerald.
The stirrups he stood on the same way were colored,
His saddle-bows too, and the studded nails splendid,
That all with green gems ever glimmered and glinted.
The horse he bestrode was in hue still the same,
Indeed;
Green, thick, and of great height,
And hard to curb, a steed
In broidered bridle bright
That such a man would need.

[*In the midst of the silence caused by this vision, King Arthur welcomes the stranger and asks him to linger. But the stranger replies that he will need only a moment to state his errand. He is not seeking a quarrel but a Christmas jest.*]

"Nay, I ask for no fight; in faith, now I tell thee
But beardless babes are about on this bench.

[2]Green growth; greenness.
[3]A leather loop passing under a horse's tail and buckled to the saddle.

Were I hasped[4] in my armor, and high on a horse,
Here is no man to match me, your might is so feeble.
So I crave but a Christmas game in this court;
Yule and New Year are come, and here men have
courage;
If one in this house himself holds so hardy,
So bold in his blood, in his brain so unbalanced
To dare stiffly strike one stroke for another,
I give this gisarme,[5] this rich axe, as a gift to him,
Heavy enough, to handle as pleases him;
Bare as I sit, I shall bide the first blow.
If a knight be so tough as to try what I tell,
Let him leap to me lightly; I leave him this weapon,
Quitclaim[6] it forever, to keep as his own;
And his stroke here, firm on this floor, I shall suffer,
This boon if thou grant'st me, the blow with another
To pay;
Yet let his respite[7] be
A twelvemonth and a day.
Come, let us quickly see
If one here aught dare say."

[*When no knight responds to the challenge, Arthur steps forward to defend the court's honor; but then Gawain begs the favor "to let this fray be mine."*]

With speed then the Green Knight took up his stand,
Inclined his head forward, uncovering the flesh,
And laid o'er his crown his locks long and lovely,
And bare left the nape of his neck for the business.
His axe Gawain seized, and swung it on high;
On the floor his left foot he planted before him,
And swiftly the naked flesh smote with his weapon.
The sharp edge severed the bones of the stranger,
Cut through the clear flesh and cleft it in twain,
So the blade of the brown steel bit the ground deeply.
The fair head fell from the neck to the floor,

4Dressed securely.
5A battle axe with the shaft ending in a spike.
6To give up any claim to it.
7Here used as intermission, interval in which to pay the debt.

So that where it rolled forth with their feet many
    spurned it.
The blood on the green glistened, burst from the body;
And yet neither fell nor faltered the hero,
But stoutly he started forth, strong in his stride;
Fiercely he rushed 'mid the ranks of the Round Table,
Seized and uplifted his lovely head straightway;
Then back to his horse went, laid hold of the bridle,
Stepped into the stirrup and strode up aloft,
His head holding fast in his hand by the hair.
And the man as soberly sat in his saddle
As if he unharmed were, although now headless,
                                        Instead.
            His trunk around he spun,
            That ugly body that bled.
            Frightened was many a one
            When he his words had said.

  For upright he holds the head in his hand,
And confronts with the face the fine folk on the dais.[8]
It lifted its lids, and looked forth directly,
Speaking this much with its mouth, as ye hear:
"Gawain, look that to go as agreed you are ready,
And seek for me faithfully, sir, till you find me,
As, heard by these heroes, you vowed in this hall.
To the Green Chapel go you, I charge you, to get
Such a stroke as you struck. You are surely deserving,
Sir knight, to be promptly repaid at the New Year.
As Knight of the Green Chapel many men know me;
If therefore to find me you try, you will fail not;
Then come, or be recreant[9] called as befits thee."
With furious wrench of the reins he turned round,
And rushed from the hall-door, his head in his hands.

II

[*The seasons pass and autumn arrives. Gawain prepares to seek out the Green Knight. He is clad in his most magnificent armor and mounts his great horse Gringolet.*]

[8]Pronounced dā'is; a raised platform or table where guests of honor are seated.
[9]Cowardly, unfaithful.

When in arms he was clasped, his costume was costly;
The least of the lacings or loops gleamed with gold.
And armed in this manner, the man heard Mass,
At the altar adored and made offering, and afterward
Came to the King and all of his courtiers,
Gently took leave of the ladies and lords;
Him they kissed and escorted, to Christ him
commending.
Then was Gringolet ready, girt with a saddle
That gaily with many a gold fringe was gleaming,
With nails studded newly, prepared for the nonce.[10]
Then they showed him his shield, sheer gules,[11]
whereon shone
The pentangle[12] painted in pure golden hue.
On his baldric[13] he caught, and about his neck cast it;
And fairly the hero's form it befitted.
And why that great prince the pentangle suited
Intend I to tell, in my tale though I tarry.
'T is a sign that Solomon formerly set
As a token, for so it doth symbol, of truth.
A figure it is that with five points is furnished;
Each line overlaps and locks in another,
Nor comes to an end; and Englishmen call it
Everywhere, hear I, the endless knot.
It became then the knight and his noble arms also,
In five ways, and five times each way still faithful.
Sir Gawain was known as the good, refined gold,
Graced with virtues of castle, of villainy void,
Made clean.
So the pentangle new
On shield and coat was seen,
As man of speech most true,
And gentlest knight of mien.°

[10]For the occasion.

[11]In heraldry, gules is a term used for the color red.

[12]A five-pointed star with interlacing lines. It was an ancient symbol of perfection. In the Middle Ages it became endowed with supernatural qualities. It was an appropriate emblem for Gawain, whose five-fold virtues were symbolized in its five sides.

[13]A belt worn diagonally across the chest and used to support a sword.

First, in his five wits he faultless was found;
In his five fingers too the man never failed;
And on earth all his faith was fixed on the five wounds
That Christ, as the creed tells, endured on the cross.
Wheresoever this man was midmost in battle,
His thought above everything else was in this,
To draw all his fire from the fivefold joys
That the fair Queen of Heaven felt in her child.
And because of this fitly he carried her image
Displayed on his shield, on its larger part,
That whenever he saw it his spirit should sink not.
The fifth five the hero made use of, I find,
More than all were his liberalness, love of his fellows,
His courtesy, chasteness, unchangeable ever,
And pity, all further traits passing. These five
In this hero more surely were set than in any.
In truth now, fivefold they were fixed in the knight,
Linked each to the other without any end,
And all of them fastened on five points unfailing;
Each side they neither united nor sundered,
Evermore endless at every angle,
Where equally either they ended or started.
And so his fair shield was adorned with this symbol,
Thus richly with red gold wrought on red gules,
So by people the pentangle perfect 't was called,
As it ought.
Gawain in arms is gay;
Right there his lance he caught,
And gave them all good-day
For ever, as he thought.

[*Sir Gawain journeys through North Wales into Cumberland in the wintry cold, struggling against serpents, wolves, wood-sprites, and giants, until he comes to wild dense wood.*]

By a mount on the morn he merrily rides
To a wood dense and deep that was wondrously wild;

High hills on each hand, with forests of hoar[14] oaks
Beneath them most huge, a hundred together.
Thickly the hazel and hawthorn were tangled,
Everywhere mantled with moss rough and ragged,
With many a bird on the bare twigs, mournful,
That piteously piped for pain of the cold.
Sir Gawain on Gringolet goes underneath them
Through many a marsh and many a mire,
Unfriended, fearing to fail in devotion,
And see not His Service, that Sire's, on that very night
Born of a Virgin to vanquish our pain.
And so sighing he said: "Lord, I beseech Thee,
And Mary, the mildest mother so dear,
For some lodging wherein to hear Mass full lowly,
And Matins,[15] meekly I ask it, to-morrow;
So promptly I pray my Pater and Ave
And Creed."
Thus rode he as he prayed,
Lamenting each misdeed;
Often the sign he made,
And said, "Christ's cross me speed."

He scarcely had signed himself thrice ere he saw
In the wood on a mound a moated mansion,
Above a fair field, enfolded in branches
Of many a huge tree hard by the ditches:
The comeliest castle that knight ever kept.
In a meadow 't was placed, with a park all about,
And a palisade,[16] spiked and pointed, set stoutly
Round many a tree for more than two miles.
The lord on that one side looked at the stronghold
That shimmered and shone through the shapely oak trees;
Then duly his helm doffed, and gave his thanks humbly
To Jesus and Julian,[17] both of them gentle,

[14]From the Anglo-Saxon *har* meaning gray or old; white or gray with age.
[15]A part of the Divine Office; in the monasteries it was sung in the early morning.
[16]A fence of stakes used for defense.
[17]Juliana of Norwich, a religious recluse venerated in the Middle Ages.

For showing him courtesy, hearing his cry.
"Now good lodging," quoth Gawain, "I beg you to grant me."
Then with spurs in his gilt heels he Gringolet strikes,
Who chooses the chief path by chance that conducted
The man to the bridge-end.

[*Gawain crosses the drawbridge and is welcomed by the lord of the castle.*]

Gawain gazed at the man who so graciously greeted him;
Doughty° he looked, the lord of that dwelling,
A hero indeed huge, hale, in his prime;
His beard broad and bright, its hue all of beaver;
Stern, and on stalwart shanks steadily standing;
Fell-faced[18] as the fire, in speech fair and free.
In sooth,[19] well suited he seemed, thought Gawain,
To govern as prince of a goodly people.

[*The lord's servants lead Gawain to richly adorned chambers where he is dressed in costly raiment. An elaborate banquet is prepared during the course of which Gawain identifies himself. After dinner, Gawain attends Vespers in the chapel, where the ladies of the castle see him for the first time.*]

Then longed the lady to look on the knight,
And emerged from her pew with many fair maidens;
In face she was fairest of all, and in figure,
In skin and in color, all bodily qualities;
Lovelier, Gawain thought, even than Guinevere.
He goes through the chancel to greet her, so gracious.
By the left hand another was leading her, older
Than she, a lady who looked as if agéd,
By heroes around her reverenced highly.
The ladies, however, unlike were to look on;

[18]Fierce.
[19]Truth.

If fresh was the younger, the other was yellow;
Rich red on the one was rioting everywhere,
Rough wrinkled cheeks hung in rolls on the other;
One's kerchiefs, with clear pearls covered and many,
Displayed both her breast and her bright throat all bare,
Shining fairer than snow on the hillsides falling;
The second her neck in a neck-cloth enswathed,
That enveloped in chalk-white veils her black chin;
Her forehead in silk was wrapped and enfolded
Adorned and tricked with trifles about it
Till nothing was bare but the lady's black brows,
Her two eyes, her nose, and her lips, all naked,
And those were bleared strangely, and ugly to see.
A goodly lady, so men before God
Might decide!
Her body thick and short,
Her hips were round and wide;
One of more pleasant sort
She led there by her side.

[*From Christmas Day to St. John's Day*[20] *mirth and joy fill the household. Gawain is pleasantly feasted and royally entertained. The next morning Gawain informs his host of his mission and asks the lord if, perhaps, he knows where the Green Knight dwells. The lord answers that the Chapel of the Green Knight is only two miles distant and can be easily reached in a few hours. He urges Gawain to remain as his guest until New Year's morning.*]

Then was Gawain right glad, and gleefully laughed.
"Now for this more than anything else, sir, I thank you.
I have come to the end of my quest; at your will
I shall bide, and in all things act as you bid me."
The lord then seized him, and set him beside him,
And sent for the ladies to better delight him.
Seemly the pleasure among them in private.
So gay were the speeches he spoke, and so friendly,
The host seemed a man well-nigh mad in behavior.

[20]December 27.

He called to the knight there, crying aloud:
"Ye have bound you to do the deed that I bid you.
Here, and at once, will you hold to your word sir?"
"Yes, certainly, sir," the true hero said;
"While I bide in your house I obey your behest."
"You have toiled," said the lord; "from afar have travelled,
And here have caroused, nor are wholly recovered
In sleep or in nourishment, know I for certain.
In your room you shall linger, and lie at your ease
To-morrow till Mass-time, and go to your meat
When you will, and with you my wife to amuse you
With company, till to the court I return.
You stay
And I shall early rise,
And hunting go my way."
Bowing in courteous wise,
Gawain grants all this play.
"And more," said the man, "let us make an agreement:
Whatever I win in the wood shall be yours;
And what chance you shall meet shall be mine in exchange.
Sir, let's so strike our bargain and swear to tell truly
Whate'er fortune brings, whether bad, sir, or better."
Quoth Gawain the good: "By God, I do grant it.
What pastime you please appears to me pleasant."

III

[*At dawn the next day the lord of the castle is off to the deer hunt. He spends the whole day in an exciting and successful chase. Meanwhile, at home, while Gawain is slumbering late in the morning, the lady comes to his chamber and attempts to make love to him. Gawain treats her with perfect courtesy and reserve and allows her to give him one kiss. In the evening, the lord returns with his catch of deer which he gives to Gawain; and in return the lord receives a kiss.*

The next day the lord hunts a wild boar. The lady again tries to make love to Gawain.]

Thus the fair lady tempted and tested him often
To make the man sin—whate'er more she'd in mind;
But so fair his defence was, no fault was apparent,
Nor evil on either side; each knew but joy
On that day.

[*In the evening the lord graciously receives two kisses from Gawain and gives the boar's head to him.*

After Mass on the next morning, the lord and his men go fox hunting:]

Wondrous fair were the fields, for the frost was clinging;
Bright red in the cloud-rack[21] rises the sun,
And full clear sails close past the clouds in the sky.
The hunters unleashed all the hounds by a woodside:
The rocks with the blast of their bugles were ringing.
Some dogs there fall on the scent where the fox is,
And trail oft a traitoress[22] using her tricks.

[*Meanwhile, at home, the lady once more visits Gawain and tempts him with her love. Courteously, without offending her in any way, Gawain refuses her attentions. He is determined not to betray the hero, the head of the house.*

The lady then gives him three kisses and begs him to receive a red gold ring. This he refuses, but she presses him to receive as a token a lace belt, "fashioned with silk, and made fair with gold."]

"Refuse ye this silk," the lady then said,
"As slight in itself? Truly it seems so,
Lo! it is little, and less is its worth;
But one knowing the nature knit up within it,
Would give it a value more great, peradventure;
For no man girt with this girdle of green,
And bearing it fairly made fast about him,
Might ever be cut down by any on earth,

[21]Collection of broken clouds drifting across the sky.
[22]The she-fox who crossed and confused the trail of the male fox.

For his life in no way in the world could be taken."
Then mused the man, and it came to his mind
In the peril appointed him precious 't would prove,
When he'd found the chapel, to face there his fortune.
The device, might he slaying evade, would be splendid.
Her suit then he suffered, and let her speak;
And the belt she offered him, earnestly urging it
(And Gawain consented), and gave it with good will,
And prayed him for her sake ne'er to display it,
But, true, from her husband to hide it. The hero
Agreed that no one should know of it ever.

[*In the evening the lord gives Gawain the skin of a fox. Gawain gives him three kisses but says nothing of the green belt.*]

IV

[*In the cold dawn of New Year's Day, Gawain arises, clothes himself in knightly armor, fastens the green belt about his waist, and accompanied by one of the lord's servants, rides off on Gringolet to find the Green Knight.*]

By hillsides where branches were bare they both
journeyed;
They climbed over cliffs where the cold was clinging.
The clouds hung aloft, but 't was lowering beneath them.
On the moor dripped the mist, on the mountains melted;
Each hill had a hat, a mist-cloak right huge.
The brooks foamed and bubbled on hillsides about
them,
And brightly broke on their banks as they rushed down.

[*The lord's servant tries to persuade Gawain from going farther, warning him that he will certainly meet his doom. Gawain refuses to heed his advice and begins his descent of the hill.*]

Rides down the rugged slope right to the dale.
Then about him he looks, and the land seems wild,

And nowhere he sees any sign of a shelter,
But slopes on each side of him, high and steep,
And rocks, gnarled and rough, and stones right rugged.
The clouds there seemed to him scraped by the crags.

[*He soon finds a mound with three openings and in it discovers the Green Chapel. Loudly he calls out:*]

"He who craves aught of me let him come hither quickly;
'T is now or never; he needs to make haste."
Said somebody, "Stop," from the slope up above him,
"And promptly you'll get what I promised to give you."
Then he came by a crag, from a cavern emerging,
Whirled out of a den with a dreadful weapon,
A new Danish axe to answer the blow with.
Said the green man, "Gawain, may God give you guard!
You are welcome indeed, sir knight, at my dwelling.
Your travel you've timed as a true man should,
And you know the compact we came to between us;
A twelvemonth ago you took what chance gave,
And I promptly at New Year was pledged to repay you."
"Nay," quoth Gawain, "by God who gave me my spirit,
I'll harbor no grudge whatever harm happens.
Exceed not one stroke and still I shall stand;
You may do as you please, I'll in no way oppose
The blow."
He left the flesh all bare,
Bending his neck down low
As if he feared naught there,
For fear he would not show.

[*The Green Knight raises his axe and brings it down, only to draw it back. Gawain has winced. A second time he lifts the great blade but withdraws it just before it enters Gawain's neck.*]

And Gawain full fiercely said in a fury:
"Come! lay on, thou dread man; too long thou art threatening.

I think that afraid of your own self you feel."
"In sooth," said the other, "thy speech is so savage
No more will I hinder thy mission nor have it
Delayed."
With puckered lips and brow
He stands with ready blade.
Not strange 't is hateful now
To him past hope of aid.
He lifts his axe lightly, and lets it down deftly,
The blade's edge next to the naked neck.
Though he mightily hammered he hurt him no more
Than to give him a slight nick that severed the skin there.

[*When Gawain sees his blood on the snow, he pulls out his sword to defend himself against a possible second stroke by the Green Knight.*]

Then gaily the Green Knight spoke in a great voice,
And said to the man in speech that resounded:
"Now be not so savage, bold sir, for towards you
None here has acted unhandsomely, save
In accord with the compact arranged in the King's court.
I promised the stroke you've received, so hold you
Well payed. I free you from all duties further.
If brisk I had been, peradventure a buffet
I'd harshly have dealt that harm would have done you.
In mirth, with a feint I menaced you first,
With no direful wound rent you; right was my deed,
By the bargain that bound us both on the first night,
When faithful and true, you fulfilled our agreement,
And gave me your gain as a good man ought to.
The second I struck at you, sir, for the morning
You kissed my fair wife and the kisses accorded me.
Two mere feints for both times I made at you, man,
Without woe.
True men restore by right,
One fears no danger so;
You failed the third time, knight,
And therefore took that blow.

"'Tis my garment you're wearing, that woven girdle,
Bestowed by my wife, as in truth I know well.
I know also your kisses and all of your acts
And my wife's advances; myself, I devised them.
I sent her to try you, and truly you seem
The most faultless of men that e'er fared on his feet.
As a pearl compared to white peas is more precious,
So next to the other gay knights is Sir Gawain.
But a little you lacked, and loyalty wanted,
Yet truly 't was not for intrigue or for wooing,
But love of your life; the less do I blame you."

[*Gawain bows his head in shame and fiercely hurls at the Green Knight the green girdle which has caused him to forsake the knightly virtue of loyalty. The Green Knight assures him that his offense has been purged and that he is spotless. He urges Gawain to come back to the castle and be his guest. Gawain refuses, but accepts the gift of the green girdle as a reminder of his failing.*]

"When in glory I move, with remorse I'll remember
The frailty and fault of the stubborn flesh,
How soon 't is infected with stains of defilement;
And thus when I'm proud of my prowess in arms,
The sight of this sash shall humble my spirit."

[*The Green Knight then informs him that he is Bercilak de Hautdesert,*[23] *lord of the castle. The whole adventure has been planned by the old woman, who is in reality Morgan le Fay,*[24] *"well versed in the crafts and cunning of magic."*]

[23]In many of the romances Bercilak occurs, but not as the Green Knight. *Hautdesert* means *hermitage in the mountains,* and refers to the Green Chapel.

[24]King Arthur's half-sister. Their mother was Igren, the Duchess of Tintagel. Gawain's mother, Anna, was another of Arthur's half-sisters. "Le Fay" means a preternatural being. In calling the old woman "le Fay," the poet gives her preternatural powers traditionally associated with Morgan; thus the old woman is linked with Celtic mythology.

"I was sent in this way to your splendid hall
To make trial of your pride, and see if the people's
Tales were true of the Table's great glory.
This wonder she sent to unsettle your wits,
And to daunt so the Queen as to cause her to die
From fear at the sight of that phantom speaker
Holding his head in his hand at the high table.
Lives she at home there, that ancient lady;
She's even thine aunt, King Arthur's half-sister."

[*Gawain rides back to Arthur's court, where, amid a royal welcome, he tells of his adventures and of his unknightly deed. But Arthur comforts the knight, and the ladies and lords of the court make this agreement:*]

That ladies and lords to the Table belonging,
All of the brotherhood, baldrics should bear
Obliquely about them, bands of bright green,
Thus following suit for the sake of the hero.
For the Round Table's glory was granted that lace,
And he held himself honored who had it thereafter,
As told in the book, the best of romances.

HONY SOYT QUI MAL PENCE.[25]

[25] This is Middle-French for the motto, "*Honi soit qui mal y pense,*" which means "shame to him who evil thinks," which is the motto of the Order of the Garter, England's oldest chivalric order. This episode of Sir Gawain and the green girdle may be connected with the foundation of the Order of the Garter in the fourteenth century.

Do especially Questions 15, 16, 17, 18, 19, 41, 49, 57, 61, 63, 65, 73, 86, 88, 89, 102, 146, 148, and 157. Consult the Model Poem on page 61.

The Canterbury Tales

GEOFFREY CHAUCER Translated by Nevill Coghill

[The first forty-two lines of the original "Prologue" are presented here in Middle English. To get the effect of Chaucer's pronunciation, the vowels should be given the following sounds: *a* is *ä; e* is *ā; i* is *ĭ; o* is *ô; ou* is *ōō;* a double vowel is always long. Final *ë* is pronounced like the final *a* in Americ*a*.]

Middle English Version

Whan that Aprille with his shourës sootë
The droghte of Marche hath percëd to the rootë,
And bathëd every veyne in swich licour,
Of which vertu engendrëd is the flour;
Whan Zephirus eek with his swetë breeth
Inspirëd hath in every holt and heeth
The tendrë croppës, and the yongë sonnë
Hath in the Ram his halfë cours y-ronnë,
And smalë fowlës maken melodyë,
That slepen al the night with open yë,
(So priketh hem nature in hir corages):
Than longen folk to goon on pilgrimages,
And palmers for to seken straungë strondës,
To fernë halwës, couthe in sondry londës;
And specially, from every shirës endë
Of Engelond, to Caunterbury they wendë,
The holy, blisful martir for to sekë,
That hem hath holpen, whan that they were sekë.
  Bifel that, in that seson on a day;
In Southwerk at the Tabard as I lay
Redy to wenden on my pilgrimagë
To Caunterbury with ful devout coragë,

At night was come i…
Wel nyne and twenty i…
Of sondry folk, by aventu… stelryë
In felawshipe, and pilgrims … nyë,
That toward Caunterbury wold… y allë,
The chambrës and the stablës we…
And wel we weren esëd attë bestë. …lë,
And shortly, whan the sonnë was to res…
So hadde I spoken with hem everichon,
That I was of hir felawshipe anon,
And madë forward erly for to rysë,
To take our wey, ther as I yow devysë.
  But natheles, whyl I have tyme and spacë,
Er that I ferther in this talë pacë,
Me thinketh it acordaunt to resoun,
To tellë yow al the condicioun
Of ech of hem, so as it semëd me,
And whiche they weren, and of what degree;
And eek in what array that they were innë:
And at a knight than wol I first biginnë.

THE PROLOGUE

When in April the sweet showers fall
And pierce the drought of March to the root, and all
The veins are bathed in liquor of such power
As brings about the engendering of the flower,
When also Zephyrus with his sweet breath
Exhales an air in every grove and heath
Upon the tender shoots, and the young sun
His half-course in the sign of the *Ram* has run,[1]
And the small fowl are making melody
That sleep away the night with open eye
(So nature pricks them and their heart engages)
Then people long to go on pilgrimages

[1]People of the Middle Ages were familiar with all the signs of the Zodiac. This was a common way of indicating early April.

And palmers long to s… anger strands
Of far-off saints, hall… sundry lands,
And specially, fro… shire's end
In England, dow… nterbury they wend
To seek the ho… ful martyr,[2] quick
To give his h… them when they were sick.
It happe… that season that one day
In Southw… at *The Tabard,* as I lay
Ready t… on pilgrimage and start
For C… rbury, most devout at heart,
At n… t there came into that hostelry
So… e nine and twenty in a company
O… sundry folk happening then to fall
…n fellowship, and they were pilgrims all
That towards Canterbury meant to ride.
The rooms and stables of the inn were wide;
They made us easy, all was of the best.
And shortly, when the sun had gone to rest,
By speaking to them all upon the trip
I soon was one of them in fellowship
And promised to rise early and take the way
To Canterbury, as you heard me say.
But none the less, while I have time and space,
Before my story takes a further pace,
It seems a reasonable thing to say
What their condition was, the full array
Of each of them, as it appeared to me
According to profession and degree,
And what apparel they were riding in;
And at a Knight I therefore will begin.

There was a *Knight,* a most distinguished man,
Who from the day on which he first began
To ride abroad had followed chivalry,
Truth, honour, generousness and courtesy.
He had done nobly in his sovereign's war
And ridden into battle, no man more,

[2] St. Thomas à Becket of Canterbury.

As well in christian as in heathen places,
And ever honoured for his noble graces.
When we took Alexandria, he was there.
He often sat at table in the chair
Of honour, above all nations, when in Prussia.
In Lithuania he had ridden, and Russia,
No christian man so often, of his rank.
When, in Granada, Algeciras sank
Under assault, he had been there, and in
North Africa, raiding Benamarin;
In Anatolia he had been as well
And fought when Ayas and Attalia fell,
For all along the Mediterranean coast
He had embarked with many a noble host.
In fifteen mortal battles he had been
And jousted for our faith at Tramissene
Thrice in the lists, and always killed his man.
This same distinguished knight had led the van
Once with the Bey of Balat, doing work
For him against another heathen Turk;
He was of sovereign value in all eyes.
And though so much distinguished, he was wise
And in his bearing modest as a maid.
He never yet a boorish thing had said
In all his life to any, come what might;
He was a true, a perfect gentle-knight.
Speaking of his equipment, he possessed
Fine horses, but he was not gaily dressed.
He wore a fustian tunic stained and dark
With smudges where his armour had left mark;
Just home from service, he had joined our ranks
To do his pilgrimage and render thanks.

He had his son with him, a fine young *Squire*,
A lover and cadet, a lad of fire
With locks as curly as if they had been pressed.
He was some twenty years of age, I guessed.
In stature he was of a moderate length,
With wonderful agility and strength.

He'd seen some service with the cavalry
In Flanders and Artois and Picardy
And had done valiantly in little space
Of time, in hope to win his lady's grace.
He was embroidered like a meadow bright
And full of freshest flowers, red and white.
Singing he was, or fluting all the day;
He was as fresh as is the month of May.
Short was his gown, the sleeves were long and wide;
He knew the way to sit a horse and ride.
He could make songs and poems and recite,
Knew how to joust and dance, to draw and write.
He loved so hotly that till dawn grew pale
He slept as little as a nightingale.
Courteous he was, lowly and serviceable,
And carved to serve his father at the table.

There was a *Yeoman* with him at his side,
No other servant; so he chose to ride.
This Yeoman wore a coat and hood of green,
And peacock-feathered arrows, bright and keen
And neatly sheathed, hung at his belt the while
—For he could dress his gear in yeoman style,
His arrows never drooped their feathers low—
And in his hand he bore a mighty bow.
His head was like a nut, his face was brown.
He knew the whole of woodcraft up and down.
A saucy brace was on his arm to ward
It from the bow-string, and a shield and sword
Hung at one side, and at the other slipped
A jaunty dirk, spear-sharp and well-equipped.
A medal of St Christopher he wore
Of shining silver on his breast, and bore
A hunting-horn, well slung and burnished clean,
That dangled from a baldrick of bright green.
He was a proper forester I guess.

There also was a *Nun*, a Prioress.
Her way of smiling very simple and coy.

Her greatest oath was only 'By St Loy!'
And she was known as Madam Eglantyne.
And well she sang a service, with a fine
Intoning through her nose, as was most seemly,
And she spoke daintily in French, extremely,
After the school of Stratford-atte-Bowe;
French in the Paris style she did not know.
At meat her manners were well taught withal;
No morsel from her lips did she let fall,
Nor dipped her fingers in the sauce too deep;
But she could carry a morsel up and keep
The smallest drop from falling on her breast.
For courtliness she had a special zest,
And she would wipe her upper lip so clean
That not a trace of grease was to be seen
Upon the cup when she had drunk; to eat,
She reached a hand sedately for the meat.
She certainly was very entertaining,
Pleasant and friendly in her ways, and straining
To counterfeit a courtly kind of grace,
A stately bearing fitting to her place,
And to seem dignified in all her dealings.
As for her sympathies and tender feelings,
She was so charitably solicitous°
She used to weep if she but saw a mouse
Caught in a trap, if it were dead or bleeding.
And she had little dogs she would be feeding
With roasted flesh, or milk, or fine white bread.
And bitterly she wept if one were dead
Or someone took a stick and made it smart;
She was all sentiment and tender heart.
Her veil was gathered in a seemly way,
Her nose was elegant, her eyes glass-grey;
Her mouth was very small, but soft and red,
Her forehead, certainly, was fair of spread,
Almost a span across the brows, I own;
She was indeed by no means undergrown.
Her cloak, I noticed, had a graceful charm.
She wore a coral trinket on her arm,

A set of beads, the gaudies[3] tricked in green,
Whence hung a golden brooch of brightest sheen
On which there first was graven a crowned A,
And lower, *Amor vincit omnia.*
  Another *Nun,* the chaplain at her cell,
Was riding with her, and *three Priests* as well.

  A *Monk* there was, one of the finest sort
Who rode the country; hunting was his sport.
A manly man, to be an Abbot able;
Many a dainty horse he had in stable.
His bridle, when he rode, a man might hear
Jingling in a whistling wind as clear,
Aye, and as loud as does the chapel bell
Where my lord Monk was Prior of the cell.
The Rule of good St Benet or St Maur
As old and strict he tended to ignore;
He let go by the things of yesterday
And took the modern world's more spacious way.
He did not rate that text at a plucked hen
Which says that hunters are not holy men
And that a monk uncloistered is a mere
Fish out of water, flapping on the pier,
That is to say a monk out of his cloister.
That was a text he held not worth an oyster;
And I agreed and said his views were sound;
Was he to study till his head went round
Poring over books in cloisters? Must he toil
As Austin bade and till the very soil?
Was he to leave the world upon the shelf?
Let Austin have his labour to himself.
  This Monk was therefore a good man to horse;
Greyhounds he had, as swift as birds, to course.
Hunting a hare or riding at a fence
Was all his fun, he spared for no expense.
I saw his sleeves were garnished at the hand
With fine grey fur, the finest in the land,

[3]Distinctive beads following each decade of a rosary.

And on his hood, to fasten it at his chin
He had a wrought-gold cunningly fashioned pin;
Into a lover's knot it seemed to pass.
His head was bald and shone like looking-glass;
So did his face, as if it had been greased.
He was a fat and personable priest;
His prominent eyeballs never seemed to settle.
They glittered like the flames beneath a kettle;
Supple his boots, his horse in fine condition.
He was a prelate fit for exhibition,
He was not pale like a tormented soul.
He liked a fat swan best, and roasted whole.
His palfrey was as brown as is a berry. . . .

An *Oxford Cleric*, still a student though,
One who had taken logic long ago,
Was there; his horse was thinner than a rake,
And he was not too fat, I undertake,
But had a hollow look, a sober stare;
The thread upon his overcoat was bare.
He had found no preferment in the church
And he was too unworldly to make search
For secular employment. By his bed
He preferred having twenty books in red
And black, of Aristotle's philosophy,
To having fine clothes, fiddle or psaltery.°
Though a philosopher, as I have told,
He had not found the stone for making gold.
Whatever money from his friends he took
He spent on learning or another book
And prayed for them most earnestly, returning
Thanks to them thus for paying for his learning.
His only care was study, and indeed
He never spoke a word more than was need,
Formal at that, respectful in the extreme,
Short, to the point, and lofty in his theme.
The thought of moral virtue filled his speech
And he would gladly learn, and gladly teach. . . .

A *Haberdasher*, a *Dyer*, a *Carpenter*,
A *Weaver* and a *Carpet-maker* were
Among our ranks, all in the livery
Of one impressive guild-fraternity.
They were so trim and fresh their gear would pass
For new. Their knives were not tricked out with brass
But wrought with purest silver, which avouches
A like display on girdles and on pouches.
Each seemed a worthy burgess, fit to grace
A guild-hall with a seat upon the dais.
Their wisdom would have justified a plan
To make each one of them an alderman;
They had the capital and revenue,
Besides their wives declared it was their due.
And if they did not think so, then they ought;
To be called '*Madam*' is a glorious thought,
And so is going to church and being seen
Having your mantle carried like a queen.

They had a *Cook* with them who stood alone
For boiling chicken with a marrow-bone,
Sharp flavouring-powder and a spice for savour.
He could distinguish London ale by flavour,
And he could roast and seethe and broil and fry,
Make good thick soup and bake a tasty pie.
But what a pity—so it seemed to me,
That he should have an ulcer on his knee.
As for blancmange, he made it with the best. . . .

A worthy *woman* from beside *Bath* city
Was with us, somewhat deaf, which was a pity.
In making cloth she showed so great a bent
She bettered those of Ypres and of Ghent.
In all the parish not a dame dared stir
Towards the altar steps in front of her,
And if indeed they did, so wrath was she
As to be quite put out of charity.
Her kerchiefs were of finely woven ground;
I dared have sworn they weighed a good ten pound,

The ones she wore on Sunday, on her head.
Her hose were of the finest scarlet red
And gartered tight; her shoes were soft and new.
Bold was her face, handsome, and red in hue.
A worthy woman all her life, what's more
She'd had five husbands, all at the church door,
Apart from other company in youth;
No need just now to speak of that, forsooth.
And she had thrice been to Jerusalem,
Seen many strange rivers and passed over them;
She'd been to Rome and also to Boulogne,
St James of Compostella and Cologne,
And she was skilled in wandering by the way.
She had gap-teeth, set widely, truth to say.
Easily on an ambling horse she sat
Well wimpled up, and on her head a hat
As broad as is a buckler or a shield;
She had a flowing mantle that concealed
Large hips, her heels spurred sharply under that.
In company she liked to laugh and chat
And knew the remedies for love's mischances,
An art in which she knew the oldest dances.

A holy-minded man of good renown
There was, and poor, the *Parson* to a town,
Yet he was rich in holy thought and work.
He also was a learned man, a clerk,
Who truly knew Christ's gospel and would preach it
Devoutly to parishioners, and teach it.
Benign and wonderfully diligent,
And patient when adversity was sent
(For so he proved in great adversity)
He much disliked extorting tithe° or fee,
Nay rather he preferred beyond a doubt
Giving to poor parishioners round about
From his own goods and Easter offerings.
He found sufficiency in little things.
Wide was his parish, with houses far asunder,
Yet he neglected not in rain or thunder,

In sickness or in grief, to pay a call
On the remotest, whether great or small,
Upon his feet, and in his hand a stave.
This noble example to his sheep he gave,
First following the word before he taught it,
And it was from the gospel he had caught it.
This little proverb he would add thereto
That if gold rust, what then will iron do?
For if a priest be foul in whom we trust
No wonder that a common man should rust; . . .
The true example that a priest should give
Is one of cleanness, how the sheep should live.
He did not set his benefice to hire
And leave his sheep encumbered in the mire
Or run to London to earn easy bread
By singing masses for the wealthy dead,
Or find some Brotherhood and get enrolled.
He stayed at home and watched over his fold
So that no wolf should make the sheep miscarry.
He was a shepherd and no mercenary.
Holy and virtuous he was, but then
Never contemptuous of sinful men,
Never disdainful, never too proud or fine,
But was discreet in teaching and benign.
His business was to show a fair behaviour
And draw men thus to Heaven and their Saviour,
Unless indeed a man were obstinate;
And such, whether of high or low estate,
He put to sharp rebuke to say the least.
I think there never was a better priest.
He sought no pomp or glory in his dealings,
No scrupulosity° had spiced his feelings.
Christ and His Twelve Apostles and their lore
He taught, but followed it himself before. . . .

Our *Host* gave us great welcome; everyone
Was given a place and supper was begun.
He served the finest victuals you could think,
The wine was strong and we were glad to drink.

A very striking man our Host withal,
And fit to be a marshal in a hall.
His eyes were bright, his girth a little wide;
There is no finer burgess in Cheapside.
Bold in his speech, yet wise and full of tact,
There was no manly attribute he lacked,
What's more he was a merry-hearted man.
After our meal he jokingly began
To talk of sport, and, among other things
After we'd settled up our reckonings,
He said as follows: 'Truly, gentlemen,
You're very welcome and I can't think when
—Upon my word I'm telling you no lie—
I've seen a gathering here that looked so spry,
No, not this year, as in this tavern now.
I'd think you up some fun if I knew how.
And, as it happens, a thought has just occurred
And it will cost you nothing, on my word.
You're off to Canterbury—well, God speed!
Blessed St Thomas answer to your need!
And I don't doubt, before the journey's done
You mean to while the time in tales and fun.
Indeed, there's little pleasure for your bones
Riding along and all as dumb as stones.
So let me then propose for your enjoyment,
Just as I said, a suitable employment.
And if my notion suits and you agree
And promise to submit yourselves to me
Playing your parts exactly as I say
Tomorrow as you ride along the way,
Then by my father's soul (and he is dead)
If you don't like it you can have my head!
Hold up your hands, and not another word.'
  Well, our consent of course was not deferred,
It seemed not worth a serious debate;
We all agreed to it at any rate
And bade him issue what commands he would.
'My lords,' he said, 'now listen for your good,
And please don't treat my notion with disdain.

This is the point. I'll make it short and plain.
Each one of you shall help to make things slip
By telling two stories on the outward trip
To Canterbury, that's what I intend,
And, on the homeward way to journey's end
Another two, tales from the days of old;
And then the man whose story is best told,
That is to say who gives the fullest measure
Of good morality and general pleasure,
He shall be given a supper, paid by all,
Here in this tavern, in this very hall,
When we come back again from Canterbury.
And in the hope to keep you bright and merry
I'll go along with you myself and ride
All at my own expense and serve as guide.
I'll be the judge, and those who won't obey
Shall pay for what we spend upon the way.
Now if you all agree to what you've heard
Tell me at once without another word,
And I will make arrangements early for it.'
  Of course we all agreed, in fact we swore it
Delightedly, and made entreaty too
That he should act as he proposed to do,
Become our Governor in short, and be
Judge of our tales and general referee,
And set the supper at a certain price.
We promised to be ruled by his advice
Come high, come low; unanimously thus
We set him up in judgement over us.
More wine was fetched, the business being done;
We drank it off and up went everyone
To bed without a moment of delay.
  Early next morning at the spring of day
Up rose our Host and roused us like a cock,
Gathering us together in a flock,
And off we rode at slightly faster pace
Than walking to St Thomas' watering-place;
And there our Host drew up, began to ease
His horse, and said, 'Now, listen if you please,

My lords! Remember what you promised me.
If evensong and mattins will agree
Let's see who shall be first to tell a tale.
And as I hope to drink good wine and ale
I'll be your judge. The rebel who disobeys,
However much the journey costs, he pays.
Now draw for cut and then we can depart;
The man who draws the shortest cut shall start. . . .

Do especially Questions 14, 32, 49, 59, 60, 67, 69, 113, 114, 133, 140, 145, and 146. Consult the Model Poem on page 61.

The Clerk's Tale

THE CLERK'S PROLOGUE

'You, sir, from Oxford!' said the Host. 'God's life!
As coy and quiet as a virgin-wife
Newly espoused and sitting mum at table!
You haven't said a word since we left stable.
Studying, I suppose? On wisdom's wing?
Says Solomon, "There's a time for everything."
'For goodness' sake cheer up, show animation!
This is no time for abstruse meditation.
Tell us a lively tale in Heaven's name;
For when a man has entered on a game
He's bound to keep the rules, it's by consent.
But don't you preach as friars do in Lent,
Dragging up all our sins to make us weep,
Nor tell a tale to send us all to sleep.
'Let it be brisk adventure, stuff that nourishes,
And not too much of your rhetorical flourishes.
Keep the "high style" until occasion brings
A use for it, like when they write to kings,
And for the present put things plainly, pray,
So we can follow all you have to say.'
This worthy cleric left the land of nod
And said benignly, 'Sir, I kiss the rod!

Our company is under your control
And I am all obedience heart and soul,
That is, as far as reason will allow.
'I heard the story I shall tell you now
In Padua, from a learned man now dead,
Of proven worth in all he did and said.
Yes, he is dead and nailed up in his chest,
And I pray God his spirit may have rest.
'Francis Petrarch,[1] the poet laureate,
They called him, whose sweet rhetoric of late
Illumined Italy with poesy,
As Lynian[2] did with his philosophy
And law, and other special kinds of learning.
Death that allows no lingering or returning
In, as it were, the twinkling of an eye
Has slain them both; and we must also die.
'But, to return to this distinguished man
From whom I learnt the tale, as I began,
Let me say first he starts it by enditing°
A preface in the highest style of writing,
Ere coming to the body of his tale,
Describing Piedmont, the Saluzzo vale,
And the high Apennines that one may see
Bounding the lands of western Lombardy;
And he is most particular to tell
Of Monte Viso, where, from a little well,
The river Po springs from its tiny source.
Eastwards it runs, increasing on its course,
Towards the Aemilian Way; Ferrara past,
It reaches Venice and the sea at last,
Which is not only far too long to tell
But, as I think, irrelevant as well,
Except to set the tale and engineer it
A frame-work. This is it, if you will hear it.'

[1]Francesco Petrarco (1304-74), the Italian poet and humanist, was made Poet Laureate at Rome in 1341. Among other things, he translated the story of Griselda into Latin from Boccaccio's *Decameron*. It is from this translation that Chaucer seems to have taken his material for the "Clerk's Tale."

[2]Giovanni di Legnano was a Professor of Law at Bologna. He wrote tracts on war and on astrology.

THE CLERK'S TALE

PART I

Upon the western shores of Italy
Where Monte Viso lifts into the cold,
There lies a plain of rich fertility
With many a town and tower to behold,
Built by their forefathers in days of old,
And other lovely things to see in legion.
Saluzzo it is called, this splendid region.

There was a marquis once who ruled that land,
As had his ancestors in days gone by.
His vassals were obedient at his hand
Ready to serve, the lowly and the high.
Honoured and dreaded, under fortune's eye
He long had lived and found the living pleasant,
Beloved alike by nobleman and peasant.

He was, moreover, speaking of descent,
The noblest-born of all in Lombardy,
Handsome and young and strong; in him were blent
High honour and a gentle courtesy.
He was discreet in his authority,
Though in some things he was indeed to blame,
As you shall hear, and Walter was his name.

I blame his failure in consideration
Of what the distant future might provide.
He always fed his present inclination,
Hawking and hunting round the countryside.
As to more serious cares, he let them slide,
And worst of all, whatever might miscarry,
He could not be prevailed upon to marry.

This was the only point that really stung them,
And so one day a deputation went
To wait on him. The wisest man among them,

Or else the least unwilling to consent
To give the marquis their admonishment,
The ablest there to touch on such a head,
Boldly addressed the marquis thus and said:

'My noble lord, your great humanity
Gives us assurance; we are therefore bold
To speak on any point of urgency
Or heavy care of which you should be told.
Then, sir, let not your clemency° withhold
A hearing to our pitiful petition;
Do not disdain my voice or our position.

'Though what I ask concerns me no more nearly
Than any of your subjects in this place,
Yet forasmuch as you have loved me dearly
And ever shown the favours of your grace,
I dare the better beg in such a case
For gentle audience; here is our request,
And you, my lord, must do as you think best.

'We love you well, sir, are indeed rejoiced
In all you do or ever did, and we
Scarce can imagine thoughts that could be voiced
To lap us round in more felicity°
Save one thing only, would that it might be!
Did you but choose, my lord, to take a wife,
What sovereign comfort to your country's life!

'O bow your neck under that blessed yoke!
It is a kingdom, not a slavery;
Espousal, wedlock, it is called. Invoke
Your wisdom, ponder carefully and see
How variously days pass; the seasons flee
Away in sleeping, waking, roaming, riding.
Time passes on and there is no abiding.

'Still in the flower of your youth's delights
Age creeps upon you, silent as a stone.

Death menaces all ages and he smites
The high and low, the known and the unknown;
We see for certain, are obliged to own
That we must die, but we are ignorant all
Of when the hour's to come, the blow to fall.

'Incline to our petition for protection,
Hear us that never crossed your least behest,°
And we, with your consent, will make election
Immediately and choose a wife possessed
Of gentlest quality and birth, the best
In all the land, beseeming to her place,
An honour both to God and to your Grace.

'Deliver us from anxious fears and rid
Our hearts of care, for blessed Jesu's sake;
For if it so befell—which God forbid!—
Your line should end, then might not fortune rake
Some strange successor in to come and take
Your heritage? Should we not all miscarry?
Therefore we beg you speedily to marry.'

Their humble prayer and their imploring features
Made much impression on his clemency
And he replied, 'My people, fellow-creatures,
Married's a thing I never thought to be.
I go rejoicing in my liberty,
And that and marriage seldom go together;
Where I was free, am I to take the tether?

'Yet, since your offer is sincerely meant,
And since I trust you now as in the past,
I freely will admit myself content
To humour you and take a wife at last.
But as for the suggestion you should cast
About to find me a bride, I must remit
That duty; kindly say no more of it.

'God knows it's true that children in the main
Are much unlike their elders gone before,

Natural goodness comes of God, no strain
Of blood can give it, no, nor ancestor;
I trust in God's good bounty; say no more.
My marriage, my condition, rank and ease
I lay on Him. Do He as He may please.

'Leave me alone to choose myself a wife,
That is my burden, my prerogative.
But I command you, charge you on your life,
That whomsoever I choose, you are to give
All honour to her, long as she may live,
In word and deed, here and elsewhere, no less
Than to an emperor's daughter or princess.

'And over this you furthermore shall swear
Never to grumble, never to check or strive
Against my choice, if I am to impair
My personal liberty that you may thrive.
Where I have set my heart I mean to wive;
If you withhold consent as to this latter
I beg you'll speak no more upon the matter.'

With heart's goodwill they gave him their assent
To this demand, not one that made objection,
But begged the princely favour ere they went
That he would name a day for the election
Of his espoused and quickly, for a section
Among his folk were yet uneasy, dreading
The marquis had no real thought of wedding.

He granted them a day of their own choosing
When he would wed in sober certainty;
He said he did so not to seem refusing
Their reasonable request, and reverently
In grave obedience then they bent the knee
Thanking him one and all, and were content,
Having achieved their aim, and home they went.

And thereupon he bade his ministers
To make such preparations as were fit

Against a feast, giving his officers
And squires such orders as he pleased for it,
And they obeyed him, setting all their wit
With diligence, the greatest and the least,
To make provision for a solemn feast.

PART II

Not far from where the noble palace stood
In which this marquis set about his wedding
There was a pretty village near a wood
Where the poor folk, each in his little steading,
Tended their animals with food and bedding
And took what sustenance they could from toil,
According to the bounty of the soil.

Among these poorer folk there dwelt a man
Who was esteemed the poorest of them all;
Yet there are times when God in Heaven can
Send grace into a little ox's stall.
Janicula the village used to call
This poor old man; his daughter was a pearl.
Griselda was the name of this young girl.

But in the virtuous beauty of her heart
She was among the loveliest man could ask,
For being poorly bred, no sensual part
Had learnt to use her beauty as a mask.
More often from the well than from the cask
She drank, and loving virtue, sought to please
By honest labour, not by idle ease.

And though as yet a girl of tender age,
Yet in the breast of her virginity
There was a ripeness, serious and sage.
With fostering love and reverent constancy
Her poor old father in his poverty
She tended, spun her wheel and watched his sheep
At pasture, never idle save asleep.

When she came homeward she would often bring
Roots, herbs and other grasses to the croft;
These she would shred and seethe for flavouring,
Then make her bed that was in nothing soft.
And thus she kept her father's heart aloft
With all the obedience, all the diligence
By which a child can show her reverence.

Griselda, though among his poorest creatures,
Walter had often seen, for, riding by,
Hunting perhaps, a something in her features
Caught his regard, not that he sought to try
The frivolous glance of wantonness; his eye
Fell on her with a serious awareness
And he would often ponder on her fairness.

Her womanliness was what his heart commended,
Her goodness too, far passing the condition
Of one so young, was beautifully blended
In looks and deeds. A vulgar intuition
Lacks insight into virtue; his position
Taught him to recognize it and decide,
Were he to marry, she should be his bride.

The day appointed for his wedding came
But no one knew what woman it should be,
In wonder at which his people would exclaim,
Talking among themselves in privacy,
'When will the marquis quit his vanity
And take a wife? Alas to see him thus!
Why does he try to fool himself and us?'

Nevertheless the marquis bade prepare
Brooches and rings, all for Griselda, lit
With jewels, gold and lapis;° he took care
Her wedding-garment should be made to fit,
But by another girl they measured it,
Who was of equal stature; gems were sewn
On it to grace a wedding like his own.

And as the morning opened on the day
Appointed when the wedding was to be,
They decked the palace out in full array,
The hall, the chambers, each in its degree:
The store-rooms, bulging with a quantity
Of delicate viands, held in plenteous strength
Italy's best from all its breadth and length.

The royal marquis in his richest dress
With lords and ladies in a company
Invited to the banquet, and no less
His household officers and soldiery,
Rode off with many a sound of minstrelsy
Towards the little thorp I spoke about
And by the shortest road, in sumptuous rout.

How could the innocent Griselda tell
That all this pomp was levelled at her head?
She had gone off for water to the well
And having drawn it, home she quickly sped,
For she had heard the marquis was to wed;
She knew it was the day and hoped she might
Be present as he passed, and see the sight.

She thought, 'I'll stand among the other girls,
My own companions, by our door and see
The marchioness, the marquis and his earls.
I'll hurry home as quickly as can be
And finish off the work that's there for me,
So that I can have leisure then to wait
And watch her riding to the castle gate.'

She reached the threshold with her water-pot
And as she did the marquis called her name.
She, putting down her vessel on the spot
Beside the cattle-stall, returned and came
Before him, falling on her knees, the same
Serious-looking girl; she knelt quite still
And waited quietly to hear his will.

The thoughtful marquis, speaking with an air
Of sober gravity, said thus to her:
'Tell me, Griselda, is your father there?'
In all humility, without demur,
She answered, 'He is here and ready, sir.'
She rose at once and of her own accord
Fetched out her father to his overlord.

He took the poor old fellow by the hand,
Leading him off to speak with him apart.
'Janicula, I can no more withstand,
No, nor conceal, the pleasures of my heart.
If you consent, accepting from the start
Whatever follows, I will take to wife
Your daughter and will love her all my life.

'You love me as I know and would obey,
Being my liege-man born and faithful too;
Whatever pleases me I dare to say
May well succeed in also pleasing you.
Yet in this point I specially pursue
Tell me, I beg you, can my purpose draw
Consent to take me for your son-in-law?'

Wholly astounded at the news he heard
The old man turned deep red and stood there quaking,
So troubled he could hardly say a word,
Except 'My lord, my will is in your making;
What you desire in any undertaking
Let me not hinder; I am bound to do,
My dear, dear master, what best pleases you.'

The marquis answered softly, 'None the less
In your own cottage you and I and she
Must have a conference. Why? You cannot guess?
I have to ask her if her will may be
To marry and submit herself to me.
This must be done while you are by to hear,
I will not speak unless I have you near.'

While they were in the chamber and about
The treaty, which you presently shall hear,
The throng pressed round their dwelling-place without
And wondered at its decency and cheer,
How well she tended on her father dear.
But she, Griseld, might wonder even more,
For such a sight she'd never seen before.

Nor is it strange Griselda was astounded
To see so great a guest in such a place,
She was not used to being so surrounded
By noble visitors. How pale her face . . .
But let me keep my story up to pace;
These are the words in which her lord conveyed
His will to this benign, true-hearted maid:

'Griselda, I would have you understand
As pleasing to your father and to me
That I should marry you, and here's my hand
If, as I may conjecture, you agree.
But I would rather ask you first,' said he,
'Since all is done in such a hasty way,
Will you consent or pause before you say?

'I warn you to be ready to obey
My lightest whim and pleasure; you must show
A willing heart, ungrudging night or day,
Whether I please to offer joy or woe.
When I say "Yes" you never shall say "No"
Either by word or frowning a defiance.
Swear this and I will swear to our alliance.'

In wonder at these words, quaking for dread,
She answered, 'Lord, unworthy though I be
Of so much honour, so unmerited,
If it seems good to you it is to me.
And here I promise never willingly
To disobey in deed or thought or breath
Though I should die, and yet I fear my death.'

'That is enough, Griselda mine!' said he.
He left the chamber then with sober tread
And reached the door; and after him came she.
And to the throng of people there he said:
'Here stands the wife it is my choice to wed.
Give her your reverence and love, I pray,
Whoever loves me. There's no more to say.'

And that she might not take the smallest bit
Of her old gear into his house, he bad
His women strip her there, and I admit
Those ladies of the court were scarcely glad
To touch the rags in which the girl was clad.
Yet the bright beauty of her natural glow
Was clothed anew at last from top to toe.

They combed her hair that fell but rudely tressed
With slender hands as if preparatory
To coronation, and a crown was pressed
Upon her head with gems of changeful glory.
Why should I let her raiment stay my story?
She stood transfigured in her gorgeous dress
Scarce recognizable for loveliness.

The marquis then espoused her with a ring
Brought for the purpose; on a horse he set her,
It was a nobly-pacing snow-white thing.
And to the palace next with those that met her,
Leading the way with joyful heart he let her
Be brought in triumph, and the day had end
In revel till they saw the sun descend.

Shortly, to let my story quicken pace,
I say this young, new marchioness so stood
In favour with the Lord and Heaven's grace
It could not seem by any likelihood
That she was born and bred in servitude,
As in a cottage or an oxen-stall,
But rather nourished in an emperor's hall.

To all that looked on her she grew so dear,
So much to be revered, where she was born
Those who had watched her childhood year by year
Could hardly credit it, and dared have sworn
That she had never laboured in the corn
Nor was Janicula's child, for by her feature
Fancy would think she was some other creature.

Virtuous ever, as had long been known,
She had increased to such an excellence
Of grace she was as bounty on a throne,
Wise, and so lovely in her eloquence,
So grave and so benign, she charmed the sense
And gathered every heart in her embrace,
They loved her all that looked upon her face.

Nor only was Griselda thus renowned
Within Saluzzo, for her bounteous name
Was published forth in all the region round.
If one said well another said the same;
Indeed her goodness had so wide a fame,
Men, women too, the younger and the older,
Went to Saluzzo only to behold her.

And thus in humble, nay, in royal kind,
Walter espoused a love as fortunate
As it was fair. God's peace was in his mind
And he enjoyed the outward gifts of fate;
And in that he had seen in low estate
The hidden grace, men held him to have been
A prudent man, and that is seldom seen.

Nor was it only that by natural wit
She could accomplish all a woman should
In homely ways, for, were there call for it,
She also could advance the public good;
There was no rancour, no discordant mood
In all that country that she did not ease
Or use her grace and wisdom to appease.

She, in her husband's absence, did not cease
Her labours; if the nobles of the land
Fell into enmity she made their peace.
So wise and ripe the words at her command,
Her heart so equitable and her hand
So just, they thought that Heaven had sent her down
To right all wrongs and to protect the town.

And it was not long after, to her joy,
Griselda bore a daughter fine and fair,
And though she would have rather borne a boy,
Walter was glad and so his people were,
For though it was a girl, perchance an heir
Might yet be born to them and likely so,
Seeing she was not barren. Time would show.

PART III

It happened, as it often does in life,
While yet the child was sucking at her breast
The marquis, in obsession for his wife,
Longed to expose her constancy to test.
He could not throw the thought away or rest,
Having a marvellous passion to assay° her.
Needless, God knows, to frighten and dismay her.

He had assayed her faith enough before
And ever found her good; what was the need
Of heaping trial on her, more and more?
Though some may praise the subtlety,° indeed
For my part I should say it could succeed
Only in evil; what could be the gain
In putting her to needless fear and pain?

But this was how he fed his prepossession;
He came alone one night to where she lay
With troubled features and a stern expression
And said, 'Griseld, do you recall the day

I came and took you from your poor array
And raised you to the height of nobleness?
You've not forgotten that, or so I guess.

'I say, Griseld, this present dignity
To which I raised you cannot have, I know,
Made you forgetful of your debt to me
Who took you up from what was poor and low,
For all the little wealth that you could show.
Take heed of every word I say to you;
No one is there to hear it but us two.

'You may remember your arrival here
Into this house, it's not so long ago;
And though I love you much and hold you dear,
My noblemen are far from doing so.
They say it is a scandal and a show
That they should serve you, lifted from the tillage
As you have been, born in a little village.

'And now you've borne your daughter, all the more
No doubt they murmur phrases such as these.
But I desire, as I did before,
To live my life among them and in ease.
I cannot then ignore contingencies°
And must dispose your daughter as is best,
Not as I wish to, but as they suggest.

'But still God knows it's painful to me too;
Yet without your full knowledge and consent
I will do nothing, but it is for you
To acquiesce and show no discontent.
Summon your patience, show that they were meant,
Those promises you gave me to obey,
Down in your village on our wedding-day.'

Apparently unmoved as she received
What he had said, no change in her expression
Or tone of voice, Griselda unaggrieved

Replied, 'My child and I are your possession
And at your pleasure; on my heart's profession
We are all yours and you may spare or kill
What is your own. Do therefore as you will.

'Nor is there anything, as God may save
My soul, that pleasing you displeases me,
Nor is there anything that I could crave
To have, or dread to lose, but you,' said she.
'This is my heart's will and shall ever be;
This may no length of time, no death deface;
My heart will never turn or change its place.'

If he were gladdened at her mild reply
There was no sign upon his face to show,
But gravely and with unrelenting eye
He gazed at her. At last he turned to go.
Soon after this, within a day or so,
He told a man in secret what he held
Was needful, and he sent him to Griseld.

He was a sort of secret agent, one
That had been ever faithful in pursuing
Important tasks. When wickedness is done
Such men are very useful in the doing.
He loved and feared his master, and reviewing
What was commanded of him, made his way
With silent stalk to where Griselda lay.

'Madam,' the fellow said, 'I must be pardoned
For doing that to which I am constrained;
You are too wise to let your heart be hardened,
You know a lord's command must be sustained
And not refused, although it be complained
Against and wept for. Servants must obey,
And so will I. There is no more to say.

'It is commanded that I take this child.'
He said no more but grabbed the innocent

Despitefully,° his countenance as wild
As if he would have slain it ere he went.
Griselda had to suffer and consent,
And like a lamb she lay there, meek and still,
And let the cruel fellow do his will.

He was a man of ominous ill-fame,
In voice and feature ominous, as are such,
And ominous the hour at which he came.
Alas, her daughter that she loved so much
Would, as she thought, be murdered at his touch.
Nevertheless she wept not nor lamented;
It was her husband's will and she consented.

She found her voice at last and she began
Humbly imploring not to be denied
This mercy, as he was a gentleman,
To let her kiss the child before it died;
She took it to her breast with terrified
And stricken face, and lulled it in her loss;
She kissed it then and signed it with the cross,

Saying with love, 'Farewell, O sacrificed
And blessed child that I shall never see;
Look, I have marked thee with the cross of Christ.
He is thy father, may He comfort thee,
Who died, for sake of us, upon a tree;
Thy little soul I offer in His sight
Since thou shalt die, for sake of me, to-night.'

And had there been a nurse with her, God knows
She would have thought it pitiful to see;
Well might a mother then have wept her woes.
Yet she was grave, and gazing steadfastly
As one who suffers all adversity
In meek submission, turned with sorrow-laden
Spirit and said, 'Take back your little maiden.

'Go now,' she said, 'and do as you are bidden.
But one thing let me beg you of your grace;

Bury the little body, be it hidden,
Unless my lord forbade it, in some place
That beasts and birds of prey can never trace.'
Yet not a word in answer would he say;
He took the little child and went his way,

Reporting to the marquis once again
What she had said, how looked, if reconciled,
As briefly point by point he made all plain
And having done he gave him up the child.
And though some touch of tenderness beguiled
His master, yet he held his purpose still
As lords will do that mean to have their will.

He bade the fellow secretly to take
The child and wrap the softest winding round
Her little form and carefully to make
A chest to bear it in; and then he bound
The man on pain of death that not a sound
Of his intention should be uttered, dumb
On whither he was going or whence come.

But to Bologna, to the marquis' sister,
The Countess of Panaro, he must go,
Taking the child, and he must there enlist her
To help him in this matter and bestow
All fostering care, so that the child might grow
In gentle grace, but above all to hide
Whose child it was, whatever should betide.

The man went off and did as he was bidden.
Now let us watch the marquis as he ranged
In quick imagination for some hidden
Sign in his wife whether she were estranged;
Was there a chance word showing she had changed
Towards him? But he still could never find
Her anything but serious and kind,

As glad, as humble and as quick to serve,
And in her love as she was wont to be;

In everything the same, she did not swerve,
And of her daughter not a word said she.
There was no sign of that adversity
To see upon her; and her daughter's name
She never used, in earnest or in game.

PART IV

Four years went by in this unaltered state
Before Griselda was with child once more,
And then she bore a boy as delicate
In grace and beauty as the child before.
The marquis, being told, set greatest store
On it; nor only he but all the county,
And all gave thanks and honour to God's bounty.

When it was two years old, weaned from the breast
And taken from its nurse, there came a day
When Walter yet again was moved to test
The patience of his wife in the same way.
O needless, needless was the test, I say!
But married men too often use no measure
That have some patient creature at their pleasure.

'Wife,' said the marquis, 'as I said at first,
My people take it ill that we were married.
Now that my son is born they think the worst;
Never were things so bad, for I am harried
By murmurings and rumours that are carried
About my ears; I feel a deadly smart
That has indeed almost destroyed my heart.

'For now they say, "When Walter's reign is done
Old Janicle's descendants will succeed
And be our masters, either that or none."
Such is the common talk, it is indeed.
Murmurs like that a ruler has to heed,
And certainly I dread all such opinions,
Though secretly advanced, in my dominions.

'I mean to live in quiet if I may,
And so am utterly disposed in mind
To serve the brother in the self-same way
As I have served his sister. I designed
To give this warning lest you were inclined
To do some outrage in your violent grief;
I beg you to be patient then, in brief.'

'I long have said,' she answered, 'Oh, believe me,
Nothing I will, nor yet would have unwilled,
But as it pleases you. It does not grieve me
At all, though son and daughter both were killed
At your commandment; let it be fulfilled.
In my two children I have had no part
But sickness first, then pain and grief of heart.

'You are our sovereign, do with what is yours
Just as you please and do not bid me frame
Advice for you; for at my father's doors
I left my clothing. Was it not the same
To leave my will and freedom when I came?
I took your clothing and I therefore pray
Your pleasure may be done. I will obey.

'And surely had I had the prescience°
To know your will before you told it me
I had performed it without negligence.
But knowing what your pleasure is to be,
I hold to it with firmest constancy.
For if I knew my death itself would ease you,
Then I would die, and gladly die, to please you.

'For death can never make comparison
Beside your love.' And when the marquis saw
Her faithfulness he could not look upon
Her face and dropped his eyes in wondering awe,
Thinking, 'What patience to endure the law
Of my caprices!' and he left the room
Happy at heart, but set his face in gloom.

The ugly officer as brutally
As he had snatched her daughter, or with more
Brutality if more in man could be,
Seized on her son, so beautiful, and tore
Him from her arms; she patient as before
Gave him no sign of suffering in her loss
But kissed her son and signed him with the cross.

But yet she begged the fellow, if he might,
To close the little body in a grave.
His tender limbs so delicate to sight
She sought in her extremity to save
From birds and beasts, but not a sign he gave
And snatched the child with careless cruelty,
But bore it to Bologna tenderly.

The marquis wondered ever more and more
At so much patience in her misery;
Had he not known for certain long before
How perfectly she loved her children, he
Would have supposed some cunning devilry
Of malice, some heart's cruelty or base
Indifference beneath her constant face.

But well the marquis knew it was no mask,
For she had ever loved her children best,
Next to himself. Now, I would like to ask
Of women, had he made sufficient test?
Could stubborn husband fancy or suggest
More that would prove a steadfast wifeliness
To one continuing stubborn to excess?

But there are folk in such a state of mind
That, if they finally resolve to take
Some certain course to which they feel inclined,
Cannot hold back, but fettered to their stake,
Hold to their purposes and cannot slake
Their fevered wills. So too this marquis nursed
His purposes, to test her as at first.

And so he waited for a word or glance
To show her change of heart, but there was none,
No variation in her countenance
Could he discover; face and heart were one.
And as she aged the love in her begun
Continued even truer, made addition,
If that could be, in love and true submission.

Therefore there seemed to be between these two
One undivided will; if Walter pressed
For something, it became her joy to do;
And God be thanked all happened for the best.
And she gave proof that in whatever test
A wife, as of herself, in nothing should
Direct her will but as her husband would.

Walter's ill-fame began to mount and spread;
His cruel soul had led him to embark
For having wed a pauper, people said,
On murdering both his children in the dark.
Such was the common murmur and remark.
No wonder if it was; by what they heard
About it, murder was the only word.

And so the love his people felt of yore
Turned into hatred; scandal and ill-fame
Are things a man may well be hated for;
To be called murderer is a hateful name.
Yet he, in game or earnest, with the same
Cruel device drove on to what he sought;
To test her further was his only thought.

Now when his daughter was some twelve years old
He sent to Rome, long cunningly apprised
Of his intentions, and the court was told
That such and such a bull° should be devised
That his fell purpose might be realized,
And that the Pope, to set all minds at rest,
Should bid him wed again, as he thought best.

I say he ordered them to counterfeit
A papal bull declaring approbation
Of a divorce, for Walter then could meet
Objection with a papal dispensation
And calm the rancour° and the indignation
Between his people and him. They framed the bull
And published the whole forgery in full.

The common people, and no wonder, held,
Or else supposed, that things were even so.
But when these tidings came to poor Griseld
I deem her heart was weighted down with woe.
But she, and now no less than long ago,
Was ready, humble creature, faithfully
To meet misfortune and adversity.

And still she waited on his will and pleasure
To whom she had been given, heart and soul,
As to her one unfailing worldly treasure.
Yet to be brief about it and control
My tale, the marquis now to reach his goal
Devised a letter that declared his aim,
And to Bologna secretly it came.

It was for Lord Panaro, for the earl
Who had espoused his sister, and requested
That he would send him home his boy and girl
In public state and openly invested
With every honour, but it still protested
That upon no account should he declare,
Even if questioned, whose the children were,

But say the maid was shortly to espouse
The Marquis of Saluzzo; and thereto
The earl agreed. As day began to rouse
He started on the journey and he drew
Towards Saluzzo with a retinue
Of many lords in rich array, to guide
This maiden and the brother at her side.

All in her wedding-dress and fresh as heaven,
She rode in pearl and gold without alloy.
Her brother too, a little lad of seven,
Looked freshly, in the tunic of a boy;
So with great splendour, every face in joy,
They shaped their journey, riding all the way;
And thus they neared Saluzzo day by day.

PART V

Meanwhile, according to his cruel bent,
The marquis sought to test his wife yet more,
And by the uttermost experiment
To prove her spirit to the very core,
Whether she still were steadfast as before;
And so in open audience one day
And in a blustering voice he chose to say:

'It was agreeable enough, forsooth,
To marry you, Griselda, in the flower
Of your obedient love and simple truth,
And not for lineage or for worldly dower;
But now I know in very truth that power,
If one reflects, is nothing much to praise;
It is a servitude in many ways.

'I may not do as any ploughman may;
My subjects are constraining me to take
Another wife, they clamour day by day.
Even the Pope has thought it fit to slake
Their rancour by consenting, you need make
No doubt of that; indeed I have to say
My second wife is now upon her way.

'Strengthen your heart to give her up your place.
As for the dowry that you brought of old,
Take it again, I grant it as a grace;
Go home, rejoin your father in his fold.
No one can count upon his luck to hold,

And I enjoin you to endure the smart
Of fortune's buffets with an even heart.'

She answered patiently without pretence:
'My lord, I know as I have always done
That, set against your high magnificence,
My poverty makes no comparison.
It cannot be denied, and I for one
Was never worthy, never in my life,
To be your chambermaid, much less your wife.

'And in this house whose lady you have made me,
As God's my witness whom I love and fear,
And as His power may gladden me and aid me,
I never thought myself the mistress here,
Rather a servant, humble and sincere,
To your high honour; so I shall think for ever
Of you, above all creatures whatsoever.

'That you so long of your benignity°
Have held me high in honour and display,
Whereas I was not worthy so to be,
I thank my God and you; and now I pray
Revoke it, for there is no more to say.
Gladly I seek my father and will live
My life with him, whatever life may give. . . .

'Touching your second wife, may God in grace
Grant you both joy and long prosperity,
For I will gladly yield her up my place
That once was such a happiness to me.
But since it pleases you, my lord,' said she,
'In whom was formerly my whole heart's rest,
Then I will go when you shall think it best.

'But as you proffer me what first I brought,
Such dowry as I had, it's in my mind
It was my wretched clothing and worth nought,
And would indeed be hard for me to find.

O blessed God, how noble and how kind
You seemed in speech, in countenance, in carriage,
That day, the day on which we made our marriage!

'It's truly said, at least I find it true
For the effect of it is proved in me,
"A love grown old is not the love once new."
And yet whatever the adversity,
Though it were death, my lord, it cannot be
That ever I should repent, though I depart,
For having wholly given you my heart.

'My lord, you know that in my father's place
You stripped me of my rags and in their stead
Gave me rich garments, as an act of grace.
I brought you nothing else it may be said
But faith and nakedness and maidenhead.
Here I return your garments and restore
My wedding-ring as well, for evermore.

'And the remainder of the gems you lent
Are in your chamber I can safely say.
Naked out of my father's house I went
And naked I return again to-day;
Gladly I'll do your pleasure, if I may.
But yet I hope you will not make a mock
Of me or send me forth without a smock. . . .'

'The smock,' he said, 'you have upon your back
You may retain; remove it to your stall.'[3]
Yet as he spoke his voice began to crack
For pity, and he turned and left the hall.
She stripped her garments in the sight of all
And in her smock, head bare and feet unshod,
Home to her father and his house she trod.

Folk followed weeping when she passed them by,
They railed on fate for all that had occurred.

[3]Janicula's cottage.

Her eyes withheld their weeping and were dry
And at this time she did not speak a word.
The news soon reached her father; when he heard
He cursed the day and hour of his birth
That fashioned him a man to live on earth.

He, never doubt it, though so old and poor,
Had ever been suspicious of the match,
Had always thought it never could endure,
In that the marquis, having had the snatch
Of his desires, would feel disgrace attach
To his estate in such a low alliance
And when he could would set it at defiance.

At her approach he hastened forth to meet her
Led by the sound of many a beholder
That wept to see her pass, and he to greet her
Brought her old cloak and cast it on her shoulder
And wept. It fitted not, for it was older
By many a day than was her wedding-dress;
The cloth was coarsely woven, comfortless.

Thus with her father for a certain space
This flower of love and wifely patience stayed.
Never a word or look upon her face
In front of others or alone conveyed
A hint that she had suffered, or betrayed
Any remembrance of her former glory;
Her countenance told nothing of her story.

And that's no wonder; in her high estate
Her spirit had a full humility,
No tender mouth for food, no delicate
Heart's hungering after royal brilliancy
Or show of pomp; benignly, patiently,
She had lived wise in honour, void of pride,
Meek and unchanging at her husband's side.

They speak of Job and his humility,
For clerics when they wish to can endite

Its praises nobly, and especially,
In men—they praise few women when they write;
Yet none can reach a humbleness as white
As women can, nor can be half so true
As women are, or else it's something new.

PART VI

Now from Bologna he of whom I spoke,
The earl, arrived. The greater and the less
Got wind of it and all the common folk
Buzzed with the news a second marchioness
Was being brought in all the loftiness
Of pomp and splendour. Such a sight to see
Had never been known in all west Lombardy.

The marquis, who had planned and knew it all,
Before the earl had fully reached his place,
Sent down for poor Griselda in her stall;
And she with humble heart and happy face
Came at his bidding, all without a trace
Of swelling thought, and went upon her knees
And greeted him with reverence and at ease.

'Griseld,' said he, 'my will is firmly set.
This maiden hither brought to be my bride
To-morrow shall as royally be met
As possible, with all I can provide
That's in my house. My servants, side by side
According to their rank, shall wait upon her
As may be best arranged in joy and honour.

'I have no woman of sufficient skill
To decorate the chambers as I hold
They should be decorated. If you will,
I should be glad to see it all controlled
By you who know me and my tastes of old.
And though your dress is not a thing of beauty,
I hope at least that you will do your duty.'

'Not only, lord, would I be glad,' said she,
'To do your will; I long and shall endeavour
To serve and please you in my own degree
And not to faint in service, now or ever.
For neither grief or happiness can sever
My love from me. My heart can never rest
Save in the ceaseless will to love you best.'

And she began upon the decorations;
There were the boards to set, the beds to make.
All she could do in many occupations
She did, and begged the maids for goodness' sake
To hurry and to sweep and dust and shake,
While she, most serviceable of them all,
Went garnishing the chambers and the hall.

The earl arrived, beginning to alight
With the two children early in the day,
And all the people ran to see the sight
Of so much opulence and rich array.
And soon among them there were those to say
That Walter was no fool, and though obsessed
To change his wife, it might be for the best.

'For she is lovelier,' they all agreed,
'And younger than Griselda. Put the case
That fruit will fall to them; a fairer breed
Will issue from such lineage and grace.'
Her brother had so beautiful a face
It caught them with delight, opinion changed
And now applauded what their lord arranged.

'O stormy people, frivolous and fickle,
Void of true judgement, turning like a vane,
Whom every novelty and rumour tickle,
How like the moon you are to wax and wane,
Clapping your praises, shouting your disdain,
False judges, dear at a penny as a rule,
Who trusts to your opinion is a fool.'

So said the serious people of the city
Who watched the throng go gazing up and down
Glad merely for the novelty, the pretty
New lady that had come to grace the town.
But let me leave the pleasure-seeking clown
And turn to my Griselda, in the press
Of all her labours, in her steadfastness.

Busy in all, she worked, disposed and settled,
Laboured and strove to cater and adorn,
Nor did she seem at all abashed or nettled
Although her clothes were coarse and somewhat torn,
But with a face as cheerful as the morn
Went to the gate with all her retinue°
To greet the marchioness, and then withdrew.

She met the guests so cheerfully and greeted them
With so much skill according to their rank
That none could find a fault in how she treated them
And all were wondering whom they had to thank,
For how could such a pauper, to be frank,
Know all the rules of honour and degree?
They praised her prudence as a rarity.

And in the meanwhile ceaselessly she still
Praised the young bride and praised her brother too
With so much heart, with such benign goodwill
That no one could have given them better due.
And in the end when all the retinue
Sat down to meat, Walter began to call
Griselda who was busy in his hall.

'Griseld,' he said to her as if in jest,
'How do you like the beauty of my wife?'
'Indeed, my lord,' she said, 'I must protest
I never saw a lovelier in my life.
God give her joy and may there be no strife
Between you, and I pray that He may send
Your fill of happiness to your lives' end!

'One thing I beg of you, and warn you too,
Never to goad her, never put on trial
This tender girl as I have known you do;
For she was fostered preciously, a vial
More delicate. I think the self-denial
Adversity might force on her would be
Harder for her to suffer than for me.'

When Walter saw this patience in Griseld,
Her happy face, no malice there at all,
And thought of his offence long upheld
To test her, ever constant as a wall,
Grave, innocent and ever at his call,
The stubborn marquis could no more repress
His pity for such wifely steadfastness.

'It is enough,' he said, 'Griselda mine!
Have no more fears, let not your heart be sore.
Your faith and gentleness as far outshine
All other faith as you were tested more,
In wealth and want, than any wife before.
Dear wife, I know your steadfastness by this.'
He took her up into his arms to kiss.

She, lost in wonder, did not seem to grasp
Or even hear the words he uttered thus,
But as a sleeper breaking from the clasp
Of an amazement, woke incredulous.°
'Griseld,' said he, 'by Him that died for us
You are my wife and I have none but you,
Nor ever had as God may judge me true!

'This is your daughter whom you so commended
As wife for me; the other on my oath
Shall be my heir as I have long intended,
They are the children of your body, both.
Bologna nourished them and fed their growth
In secret; take them back and never say
Your children have been lost or snatched away.

'Let those that otherwise have talked of me
Know that I did this, be it bad or good,
Neither in malice nor in cruelty
But for the trial of your womanhood.
What! Slay my children? God forbid I should!
Rather I kept them privately apart
Till I had proved the purpose of your heart.'

On hearing this Griselda fell aswoon
In piteous joy, but made recovery
And called her children to her and they soon
Were folded in her arms. How tenderly
She kissed them as the salt tears falling free
Bathed them and glistened on their face and hair;
How like a mother stood Griselda there!

And Oh how pitiful it was to see
Her fainting and to hear her humble tone,
'All thanks to you, my dearest lord,' said she,
'For you have saved my children, you alone!
Were I to die this moment I have known
Your love and have found favour in your sight,
And death were nothing, though I died to-night.

'O dear, O tender ones, so long away,
Your sorrowing mother steadfastly had thought
That some foul vermin, hound or beast of prey
Had eaten you. But God in mercy brought
You back to me and your kind father sought
In tender love to keep you safe and sound.'
She suddenly swooned again and fell to ground.

Though she had fainted, sadly, clingingly
She held her children in that first embrace,
And it was difficult for skill to free
Them from her arms, and touching to unlace.
O many a tear on many a pitying face
Ran down among those standing at her side,
Scarce able in her presence to abide.

Walter caressed her, loosed her from her grief,
And up she rose bewildered from her trance,
While all the rest in joy at her relief
Made much of her and cleared her countenance;
And Walter showed such loving vigilance
It was a dainty thing to see the air
Of new-found happiness between the pair.

The ladies round her, when the moment came,
Led her towards her chamber; there the old
Poor rags she wore, though never worn in shame,
They stripped and set on her a gown of gold;
A coronet of jewels manifold
They crowned her with and led her into hall
There to receive the homage of them all.

Thus to a piteous day a blissful close,
And every man and woman, as they might,
Gave themselves up to revelry; there rose
The stars and all the welkin° shone with light.
Greater the glad solemnities that night,
Greater the joy in feasting and defray
In treasure than upon their wedding-day.

For many a year in high prosperity
These two lived on in concord to the close;
Their daughter too they married worthily
And richly to a lord, best among those
In Italy. They also found repose
For old Janicula whom Walter kept
Safe at his court till soul from body crept.

Their son succeeded to the inheritance
After his father's day in peace and rest;
He married happily but did not chance
To put his wife to such a searching test.
This world of ours, it has to be confessed,
Is not so sturdy as it was of old.
Hear how my author ends the tale he told:

'This story does not mean it would be good
For wives to ape Griseld's humility,
It would be unendurable they should.
But everybody in his own degree
Should be as perfect in his constancy
As was Griselda.' That is why Petrarch chose
To tell her story in his noble prose.

For since a woman showed such patience to
A mortal man, how much the more we ought
To take in patience all that God may do!
Reason He has to test what He has wrought,
Yet never tempts the souls that He has bought
Above what they are able, and St James
Tells us He tests us daily, and reclaims.

He will permit, to exercise our virtue,
The sharper scourges of adversity
To lash us often, not that they may hurt you,
Nor yet to test the will, for certainly
No one can know our frailty more than He
Who knew them ere our birth, and all is best;
Then let our virtues learn to suffer test.

But one word more, my lords, before I go.
It isn't very easy nowadays
To find Griseldas round the town, you know.
And if you try imposing these assays,
What gold they have is mixed with such allays
Of brass, that though the coin looks right perhaps,
When you begin to bend the thing, it snaps.

So, from affection for the Wife of Bath,
Whose life and all her sect may God maintain
In high authority upon their path
—And pity else—I sing you this refrain
With lusty heart, to gladden you again,
Dropping the note of earnest emphasis.
So listen to my song, it goes like this:

CHAUCER'S ENVOY TO THE CLERK'S TALE

Griselda and her patience both are dead
And buried in some far Italian vale.
So let it then in open court be said,
'Husbands, be not so hardy as to assail
The patience of your wives in hope to find
Griseldas, for you certainly will fail.

O noble wives, in highest prudence bred,
Allow no such humility to nail
Your tongues, or give a scholar cause to shed
Such light on you as this astounding tale
Sheds on Griselda, patient still and kind,
Lest Chichevache[4] engulf you like a whale.

Imitate Echo, she that never fled
In silence, but returns you hail for hail,
Never let innocence besot your head,
But take the helm yourselves and trim the sail,
And print this lesson firmly in your mind
For common profit; it can never stale.

Arch-wives, stand up, defend your board and bed!
Stronger than camels as you are, prevail!
Don't swallow insults, offer them instead.
And all you slender little wives and frail,
Be fierce as Indian tigers, since designed
To rattle like a windmill in a gale.

Never revere them, never be in dread,
For though your husband wears a coat of mail
Your shafts of crabbed eloquence will thread
His armour through and drub him like a flail,

[4]The reference here is to an old French fable in which there were two cows named Chichevache and Bicorne. Bicorne was fat because she made her diet on patient husbands, who were in plentiful supply. But poor Chichevache was thin, for her diet was only patient wives.

Voice your suspicions of him! Guilt will bind
Him down, he'll couch as quiet as a quail.

If you are beautiful, advance your tread,
Show yourself off to people, blaze the trail!
If you are ugly, spend and make a spread,
Get friends, they'll do the business of a male;
Dance like a linden-leaf if so inclined,
Leave him to weep and wring his hands and wail!'

Do especially Questions 3, 41, 67, 70, 73, 74, 76, 83, 86, 90, 95, 102, 103, 117, and 157. Consult the Model Poem on page 61.

GEOFFREY CHAUCER *1340?-1400*

Geoffrey Chaucer was a many-sided personality; a loyal churchman, a well-mannered courtier and successful diplomat, a competent businessman, a sharp observer of all the many types of people he met. He knew French and Italian literature, the ancient classics, and the complex scientific writings of his day. All of this experience he used in the books he wrote. One of his many strong points is irony. He gives a picture of himself in the *Canterbury Tales* as short and dumpy, rather gloomy, but with "something elvish in his countenance." Although he has assigned to the other characters tales that are unsurpassed in Middle English literature, the story he has himself telling is a boring imitation of the worst of the many medieval romances. Before Chaucer's own tale has hardly begun, the Host breaks in: "No more of this for God's dear dignity! You're wearying me to death, I say, with your illiterate stuff. . . . The devil take such rhymes! They're purgatory!"

Everyman

Characters

GOD

MESSENGER	KNOWLEDGE
DEATH	CONFESSION
EVERYMAN	BEAUTY
FELLOWSHIP	STRENGTH
KINDRED	DISCRETION
COUSIN	FIVE WITS
GOODS	ANGEL
GOOD DEEDS	DOCTOR

Here beginneth a treatise how the High Father of Heaven sendeth Death to summon every creature to come and give account of their lives in this world, and is in manner of a moral play.

MESSENGER. I pray you all give your audience,
And hear this matter with reverence,
By figure a moral play:
The *Summoning of Everyman* called it is,
That of our lives and ending shows
How transitory° we be all day.
This matter is wondrous precious,
But the intent of it is more gracious,[1]
And sweet to bear away.
The story saith: Man, in the beginning
Look well, and take good heed to the ending,
Be you never so gay!
Ye think sin in the beginning full sweet,
Which in the end causeth the soul to weep,
When the body lieth in clay.
Here shall you see how Fellowship and Jollity,
Both Strength, Pleasure, and Beauty,
Will fade from thee as flower in May;
For ye shall hear how our Heaven King

[1]A pun on "pleasing" and "grace-bringing."

Calleth Everyman to a general reckoning:
Give audience, and hear what he doth say. [*Exit.*]

[GOD *speaketh:*]

GOD. I perceive, here in my majesty,
How that all creatures be to me unkind,
Living without dread in worldly prosperity:
Of ghostly[2] sight the people be so blind,
Drowned in sin, they know me not for their God;
In worldly riches is all their mind,
They fear not my righteousness, the sharp rod.
My law that I showed, when I for them died,
They forget clean, and shedding of my blood red;
I hanged between two, it cannot be denied;
To get them life I suffered to be dead;
I healed their feet, with thorns hurt was my head.
I could do no more than I did, truly;
And now I see the people do clean forsake me:
They use the seven deadly sins damnable,
As pride, covetise, wrath, and lechery
Now in the world be made commendable;
And thus they leave of angels the heavenly company.
Every man liveth so after his own pleasure,
And yet of their life they be nothing sure:
I see the more that I them forbear
The worse they be from year to year.
All that liveth appaireth[3] fast;
Therefore I will, in all the haste,
Have a reckoning of every man's person;
For, and I leave the people thus alone
In their life and wicked tempests,
Verily they will become much worse than beasts;
For now one would by envy another up eat;
Charity they do all clean forget.
I hoped well that every man
In my glory should make his mansion,

[2]Spiritual.
[3]Dissolves, degenerates.

And thereto I had them all elect;
But now I see, like traitors deject,
They thank me not for the pleasure that I to them meant,
Nor yet for their being that I them have lent.
I proffered the people great multitude of mercy,
And few there be that asketh it heartily.
They be so cumbered with worldly riches
That needs on them I must do justice,
On every man living without fear.
Where art thou, Death, thou mighty messenger?

[*Enter* DEATH.]

DEATH. Almighty God, I am here at your will,
Your commandment to fulfil.
GOD. Go thou to Everyman,
And show him, in my name,
A pilgrimage he must on him take,
Which he in no wise may escape;
And that he bring with him a sure reckoning
Without delay or any tarrying. [GOD *withdraws.*]
DEATH. Lord, I will in the world go run overall,
And cruelly outsearch both great and small;
Every man will I beset that liveth beastly
Out of God's laws, and dreadeth not folly.
He that loveth riches I will strike with my dart,
His sight to blind, and from heaven to depart—
Except that alms be his good friend—
In hell for to dwell, world without end.
Lo, yonder I see Everyman walking.
Full little he thinketh on my coming;
His mind is on fleshly lusts and his treasure,
And great pain it shall cause him to endure
Before the Lord, Heaven King.

[*Enter* EVERYMAN.]

Everyman, stand still! Whither art thou going
Thus gaily? Hast thou thy Maker forget?

EVERYMAN. Why askest thou?
Wouldest thou wit?[4]
DEATH. Yea, sir; I will show you:
In great haste I am sent to thee
From God out of his majesty.
EVERYMAN. What, sent to me?
DEATH. Yea, certainly.
Though thou have forget him here,
He thinketh on thee in the heavenly sphere,
As, ere we depart, thou shalt know.
EVERYMAN. What desireth God of me?
DEATH. That shall I show thee:
A reckoning he will needs have
Without any longer respite.°
EVERYMAN. To give a reckoning longer leisure I crave;
This blind matter troubleth my wit.
DEATH. On thee thou must take a long journey;
Therefore thy book of count with thee thou bring,
For turn again[5] thou cannot by no way.
And look thou be sure of thy reckoning,
For before God thou shalt answer, and show
Thy many bad deeds, and good but a few;
How thou has spent thy life, and in what wise,
Before the chief Lord of paradise.
Have ado that we were in that way,
For, wit thou well, thou shalt make none attorney.
EVERYMAN. Full unready I am such reckoning to give.
I know thee not. What messenger art thou?
DEATH. I am Death, that no man dreadeth,[6]
For every man I rest,[7] and no man spareth;
For it is God's commandment
That all to me should be obedient.
EVERYMAN. O Death, thou comest when I had thee least in mind!
In thy power it lieth me to save;
Yet of my good will I give thee, if thou will be kind:

[4]Know.
[5]Return.
[6]THAT NO MAN DREADETH—That is, I, Death, fear no man.
[7]Arrest, seize.

Yea, a thousand pound shalt thou have,
And defer this matter till another day.
DEATH. Everyman, it may not be, by no way.
I set not by gold, silver, nor riches,
Ne by pope, emperor, king, duke, ne princes;
For, and[8] I would receive gifts great,
All the world I might get;
But my custom is clean contrary.
I give thee no respite. Come hence, and not tarry.
EVERYMAN. Alas, shall I have no longer respite?
I may say Death giveth no warning!
To think on thee, it maketh my heart sick,
For all unready is my book of reckoning.
But twelve year and I might have abiding,[9]
My counting-book I would make so clear
That my reckoning I should not need to fear.
Wherefore, Death, I pray thee, for God's mercy,
Spare me till I be provided of remedy.
DEATH. Thee availeth not to cry, weep, and pray;
But haste thee lightly that thou were gone that journey,
And prove thy friends if thou can;
For, wit thou well, the tide abideth no man,
And in the world each living creature
For Adam's sin must die of nature.
EVERYMAN. Death, if I should this pilgrimage take,
And my reckoning surely make,
Show me, for saint charity,
Should I not come again shortly?
DEATH. No, Everyman; and thou be once there,
Thou mayst never more come here,
Trust me verily.
EVERYMAN. O gracious God in the high seat celestial,
Have mercy on me in this most need!
Shall I have no company from this vale terrestrial°
Of mine acquaintance, that way me to lead?
DEATH. Yea, if any be so hardy
That would go with thee and bear thee company.

[8] If.
[9] If only I could live for twelve more years.

Hie thee[10] that thou were gone to God's magnificence,
Thy reckoning to give before his presence.
What, weenest thou[11] thy life is given thee,
And thy worldly goods also?
EVERYMAN. I had wend so, verily.
DEATH. Nay, nay; it was but lent thee;
For as soon as thou art go,
Another a while shall have it, and then go therefro,
Even as thou hast done.
Everyman, thou art mad! Thou hast thy wits five,
And here on earth will not amend thy life;
For suddenly I do come.
EVERYMAN. O wretched caitiff,° whither shall I flee,
That I might scape this endless sorrow?
Now, gentle Death, spare me till tomorrow,
That I may amend me
With good advisement.
DEATH. Nay, thereto I will not consent,
Nor no man will I respite;
But to the heart suddenly I shall smite
Without any advisement.
And now out of thy sight I will me hie;
See thou make thee ready shortly,
For thou mayst say this is the day
That no man living may scape away. [*Exit* DEATH.]
EVERYMAN. Alas, I may well weep with sighs deep!
Now have I no manner of company
To help me in my journey, and me to keep;
And also my writing is full unready.
How shall I do now for to excuse me?
I would to God I had never be get![12]
To my soul a full great profit it had be;
For now I fear pains huge and great.
The time passeth. Lord, help, that all wrought!
For though I mourn it availeth nought.
The day passeth, and is almost ago;

[10] Hurry up.
[11] Do you suppose.
[12] Been born.

I wot not well what for to do.
To whom were I best my complaint to make?
What and I to Fellowship thereof spake,
And showed him of this sudden chance?
For in him is all mine affiance;[13]
We have in the world so many a day
Be good friends in sport and play.
I see him yonder, certainly.
I trust that he will bear me company;
Therefore to him will I speak to ease my sorrow.
Well met, good Fellowship, and good morrow!

[FELLOWSHIP *speaketh:*]

FELLOWSHIP. Everyman, good morrow, by this day!
Sir, why lookest thou so piteously?
If any thing be amiss, I pray thee me say,
That I may help to remedy.
EVERYMAN. Yea, good Fellowship, yea;
I am in great jeopardy.
FELLOWSHIP. My true friend, show to me your mind;
I will not forsake thee to my life's end,
In the way of good company.
EVERYMAN. That was well spoken, and lovingly.
FELLOWSHIP. Sir, I must needs know your heaviness;
I have pity to see you in any distress.
If any have you wronged, ye shall revenged be,
Though I on the ground be slain for thee—
Though that[14] I know before that I should die.
EVERYMAN. Verily, Fellowship, gramercy.[15]
FELLOWSHIP. Tush! by thy thanks I set not a straw.
Show me your grief, and say no more.
EVERYMAN. If I my heart should to you break,
And then you to turn your mind from me,
And would not me comfort when ye hear me speak,
Then should I ten times sorrier be.
FELLOWSHIP. Sir, I say as I will do indeed.

[13]Trust.
[14]Even though.
[15]GRAMERCY—From the French, *grand-merci*, thanks.

EVERYMAN. Then be you a good friend at need:
I have found you true herebefore.
FELLOWSHIP. And so ye shall evermore;
For, in faith, and thou go to hell,
I will not forsake thee by the way.
EVERYMAN. Ye speak like a good friend;
I believe you well.
I shall deserve it, and I may.
FELLOWSHIP. I speak of no deserving, by this day!
For he that will say, and nothing do,
Is not worthy with good company to go;
Therefore show me the grief of your mind,
As to your friend most loving and kind.
EVERYMAN. I shall show you how it is:
Commanded I am to go a journey,
A long way, hard and dangerous,
And give a strait count, without delay,
Before the high Judge, Adonai.[16]
Wherefore, I pray you, bear me company,
As ye have promised, in this journey.
FELLOWSHIP. That is matter indeed. Promise is duty;
But, and I should take such a voyage on me,
I know it well, it should be to my pain;
Also it maketh me afeard, certain.
But let us take counsel here as well as we can,
For your words would fear a strong man.
EVERYMAN. Why, ye said if I had need
Ye would me never forsake, quick ne dead,
Though it were to hell, truly.
FELLOWSHIP. So I said, certainly,
But such pleasures be set aside, the sooth to say;
And also, if we took such a journey,
When should we come again?
EVERYMAN. Nay, never again, till the day of doom.
FELLOWSHIP. In faith, then will not I come there!
Who hath you these tidings brought?
EVERYMAN. Indeed, Death was with me here.

[16]Old Testament name for God.

FELLOWSHIP. Now, by God that all hath bought,
If Death were the messenger,
For no man that is living today
I will not go that loath journey—
Not for the father that begat me!
EVERYMAN. Ye promised otherwise, pardie.[17]
FELLOWSHIP. I wot well I said so, truly;
And yet if thou wilt eat, and drink, and make good cheer,
Or haunt to women the lusty company,
I would not forsake you while the day is clear,
Trust me verily.
EVERYMAN. Yea, thereto ye would be ready!
To go to mirth, solace, and play,
Your mind will sooner apply,
Than to bear me company in my long journey.
FELLOWSHIP. Now, in good faith, I will not that way.
But and thou will murder, or any man kill,
In that I will help thee with a good will.
EVERYMAN. O, that is a simple advice indeed.
Gentle fellow, help me in my necessity!
We have loved long, and now I need;
And now, gentle Fellowship, remember me.
FELLOWSHIP. Whether ye have loved me or no,
By Saint John, I will not with thee go.
EVERYMAN. Yet, I pray thee, take the labour, and do so much for me
To bring me forward, for saint charity,
And comfort me till I come without the town.
FELLOWSHIP. Nay, and thou would give me a new gown,
I will not a foot with thee go;
But, and thou had tarried, I would not have left thee so.
And as now God speed thee in thy journey,
For from thee I will depart as fast as I may.
EVERYMAN. Whither away, Fellowship? Will thou forsake me?

[17]From the French, *Pardieu*, a mild oath.

FELLOWSHIP. Yea, by my fay!° To God I betake thee.
EVERYMAN. Farewell, good Fellowship; for thee my heart is sore.
Adieu for ever! I shall see thee no more.
FELLOWSHIP. In faith, Everyman, farewell now at the ending;
For you I will remember that parting is mourning.

[*Exit* FELLOWSHIP.]

EVERYMAN. Alack! shall we thus depart indeed—
Ah, Lady, help!—without any more comfort?
Lo, Fellowship forsaketh me in my most need.
For help in this world whither shall I resort?
Fellowship herebefore with me would merry make,
And now little sorrow for me doth he take.
It is said, "In prosperity men friends may find,
Which in adversity be full unkind."
Now whither for succour shall I flee,
Sith that Fellowship hath forsaken me?
To my kinsmen I will, truly,
Praying them to help me in my necessity;
I believe that they will do so,
For kind[18] will creep where it may not go.
I will go say,[19] for yonder I see them.
Where be ye now, my friends and kinsmen?

[*Enter* KINDRED *and* COUSIN.]

KINDRED. Here be we now at your commandment.
Cousin, I pray you show us your intent
In any wise, and do not spare.
COUSIN. Yea, Everyman, and to us declare
If ye be disposed to go anywhither;
For, wit you well, we will live and die together.
KINDRED. In wealth and woe we will with you hold,
For over his kin a man may be bold.
EVERYMAN. Gramercy, my friends and kinsmen kind.

[18]Kindred.
[19]Essay, try.

Now shall I show you the grief of my mind:
I was commanded by a messenger,
That is a high king's chief officer;
He bade me go a pilgrimage, to my pain,
And I know well I shall never come again;
Also I must give a reckoning strait,
For I have a great enemy that hath me in wait,
Which intendeth me for to hinder.

KINDRED. What account is that which ye must render?
That would I know.

EVERYMAN. Of all my works I must show
How I have lived and my days spent;
Also of ill deeds that I have used
In my time, sith life was me lent;
And of all virtues that I have refused.
Therefore, I pray you, go thither with me
To help to make mine account, for saint charity.

COUSIN. What, to go thither? Is that the matter?
Nay, Everyman, I had liefer fast bread and water
All this five year and more.

EVERYMAN. Alas, that ever I was bore!
For now shall I never be merry,
If that you forsake me.

KINDRED. Ah, sir, what ye be a merry man!
Take good heart to you, and make no moan.
But one thing I warn you, by Saint Anne—
As for me, ye shall go alone.

EVERYMAN. My Cousin, will you not with me go?

COUSIN. No, by our Lady! I have the cramp in my toe.
Trust not to me, for, so God me speed,
I will deceive you in your most need.

KINDRED. It availeth not us to tice.[20]
Ye shall have my maid with all my heart;
She loveth to go to feasts, there to be nice,
And to dance, and abroad to start:
I will give her leave to help you in that journey,
If that you and she may agree.

[20]IT AVAILETH . . . TICE—No use trying to entice us.

EVERYMAN. Now show me the very effect
of your mind:
Will you go with me, or abide behind?
KINDRED. Abide behind? Yea, that will I, and I may!
Therefore farewell till another day. [*Exit* KINDRED.]
EVERYMAN. How should I be merry or glad?
For fair promises men to me make,
But when I have most need they me forsake.
I am deceived; that maketh me sad.
COUSIN. Cousin Everyman, farewell now,
For verily I will not go with you.
Also of mine own an unready reckoning
I have to account; therefore I make tarrying.
Now God keep thee, for now I go. [*Exit* COUSIN.]
EVERYMAN. Ah, Jesus, is all come hereto?
Lo, fair words maketh fools fain;
They promise, and nothing will do, certain.
My kinsmen promised me faithfully
For to abide with me steadfastly,
And now fast away do they flee:
Even so Fellowship promised me.
What friend were best me of to provide?
I lose my time here longer to abide.
Yet in my mind a thing there is:
All my life I have loved riches;
If that my Good now help me might,
He would make my heart full light.
I will speak to him in this distress—
Where art thou, my Goods and riches?

[GOODS *speaks from a corner:*]

GOODS. Who calleth me? Everyman? What!
hast thou haste?
I lie here in corners, trussed and piled so high,
And in chests I am locked so fast,
Also sacked in bags. Thou mayst see with thine eye
I cannot stir; in packs low I lie.
What would ye have? Lightly me say.

EVERYMAN. Come hither, Good, in all the haste thou may,
For of counsel I must desire thee.
GOODS. Sir, and ye in the world have sorrow or adversity,
That can I help you to remedy shortly.
EVERYMAN. It is another disease that grieveth me;
In this world it is not, I tell thee so.
I am sent for, another way to go,
To give a strait count general
Before the highest Jupiter of all;
And all my life I have had joy and pleasure in thee,
Therefore, I pray thee, go with me;
For, peradventure, thou mayst before God Almighty
My reckoning help to clean and purify;
For it is said ever among
That money maketh all right that is wrong.
GOODS. Nay, Everyman, I sing another song.
I follow no man in such voyages;
For, and I went with thee,
Thou shouldst fare much the worse for me;
For because on me thou did set thy mind,
Thy reckoning I have made blotted and blind,
That thine account thou cannot make truly;
And that hast thou for the love of me.
EVERYMAN. That would grieve me full sore,
When I should come to that fearful answer.
Up, let us go thither together.
GOODS. Nay, not so! I am too brittle, I may not endure;
I will follow no man one foot, be ye sure.
EVERYMAN. Alas, I have thee loved, and had great pleasure
All my life-days on good and treasure.
GOODS. That is to thy damnation, without leasing,[21]
For my love is contrary to the love everlasting;
But if thou had me loved moderately during,
As to the poor to give part of me,

[21]Without lying.

Then shouldst thou not in this dolour° be,
Nor in this great sorrow and care.
EVERYMAN. Lo, now was I deceived ere I was ware,
And all I may wite misspending of time.[22]
GOODS. What, weenest thou that I am thine?
EVERYMAN. I had wend so.
GOODS. Nay, Everyman, I say no.
As for a while I was lent thee;
A season thou hast had me in prosperity.
My condition is man's soul to kill;
If I save one, a thousand I do spill.
Weenest thou that I will follow thee?
Nay, not from this world, verily.
EVERYMAN. I had wend otherwise.
GOODS. Therefore to thy soul Good is a thief;
For when thou art dead, this is my guise—
Another to deceive in this same wise
As I have done thee, and all to his soul's reprief.[23]
EVERYMAN. O false Good, cursed may thou be,
Thou traitor to God, that hast deceived me
And caught me in thy snare!
GOODS. Marry, thou brought thyself in care,
Whereof I am glad;
I must needs laugh, I cannot be sad.
EVERYMAN. Ah, Good, thou hast had long my heartly love;
I gave thee that which should be the Lord's above.
But wilt thou not go with me indeed?
I pray thee truth to say.
GOODS. No, so God me speed!
Therefore farewell, and have good day.

[*Exit* GOODS.]

EVERYMAN. O, to whom shall I make my moan
For to go with me in that heavy journey?
First Fellowship said he would with me gone;
His words were very pleasant and gay,

[22]I may consider it all as misspent time.
[23]Disgrace.

But afterward he left me alone.
Then spake I to my kinsmen, all in despair,
And also they gave me words fair;
They lacked no fair speaking,
But all forsook me in the ending.
Then went I to my Goods, that I loved best,
In hope to have comfort, but there had I least;
For my Goods sharply did me tell
That he bringeth many into hell.
Then of myself I was ashamed,
And so I am worthy to be blamed;
Thus may I well myself hate.
Of whom shall I now counsel take?
I think that I shall never speed
Till that I go to my Good Deed.
But, alas, she is so weak
That she can neither go nor speak;
Yet will I venture on her now.
My Good Deeds, where be you?

[GOOD DEEDS *speaks from the ground:*]

GOOD DEEDS. Here I lie, cold in the ground;
Thy sins hath me sore bound,
That I cannot stir.

EVERYMAN. O Good Deeds, I stand in fear!
I must you pray of counsel,
For help now should come right well.

GOOD DEEDS. Everyman, I have understanding
That ye be summoned account to make
Before Messias, of Jerusalem King;
And you do by me,[24] that journey with you will I take.

EVERYMAN. Therefore I come to you, my moan to make;
I pray you that ye will go with me.

GOOD DEEDS. I would full fain, but I cannot stand, verily.

EVERYMAN. Why, is there anything on you fall?[25]

[24]DO BY ME—Do as I say.
[25]IS . . . FALL—Has anything happened to you?

GOOD DEEDS. Yea, sir, I may thank you of all;
If ye had perfectly cheered me,
Your book of count full ready had be.
Look, the books of your works and deeds eke![26]
Behold how they lie under the feet,
To your soul's heaviness.
EVERYMAN. Our Lord Jesus help me!
For one letter here I cannot see.
GOOD DEEDS. There is a blind reckoning in time of distress.
EVERYMAN. Good Deeds, I pray you help me in this need,
Or else I am for ever damned indeed;
Therefore help me to make reckoning
Before the Redeemer of all thing,
That King is, and was, and ever shall.
GOOD DEEDS. Everyman, I am sorry of your fall,
And fain would I help you, and I were able.
EVERYMAN. Good Deeds, your counsel I pray you give me.
GOOD DEEDS. That shall I do verily;
Though that on my feet I may not go,
I have a sister that shall with you also,
Called Knowledge, which shall with you abide,
To help you to make that dreadful reckoning.

[*Enter* KNOWLEDGE.]

KNOWLEDGE. Everyman, I will go with thee, and be thy guide,
In thy most need to go by thy side.
EVERYMAN. In good condition I am now in everything,
And am wholly content with this good thing,
Thanked be God my creator.
GOOD DEEDS. And when she hath brought you there
Where thou shalt heal thee of thy smart,
Then go you with your reckoning and your Good Deeds together,

[26]Also.

For to make you joyful at heart
Before the blessed Trinity.
EVERYMAN. My Good Deeds, gramercy!
I am well content, certainly,
With your words sweet.
KNOWLEDGE. Now go we together lovingly
To Confession, that cleansing river.
EVERYMAN. For joy I weep; I would we were there!
But, I pray you, give me cognition°
Where dwelleth that holy man, Confession.
KNOWLEDGE. In the house of salvation:
We shall find him in that place,
That shall us comfort, by God's grace.

[KNOWLEDGE *takes* EVERYMAN *to* CONFESSION.]

Lo, this is Confession; kneel down and ask mercy,
For he is in good conceit with God Almighty.
EVERYMAN. O glorious fountain, that all uncleanness doth clarify,
Wash from me the spots of vice unclean,
That on me no sin may be seen.
I come with Knowledge for my redemption,
Redempt with heart and full contrition;
For I am commanded a pilgrimage to take,
And great accounts before God to make.
Now I pray you, Shrift, mother of salvation,
Help my Good Deeds for my piteous exclamation.
CONFESSION. I know your sorrow well, Everyman.
Because with Knowledge ye come to me,
I will you comfort as well as I can,
And a precious jewel I will give thee,
Called penance, voider of adversity;
Therewith shall your body chastised be,
With abstinence and perseverance in God's service.
Here shall you receive that scourge of me,
Which is penance strong that ye must endure,
To remember thy Saviour was scourged for thee
With sharp scourges, and suffered it patiently;
So must thou, ere thou scape that painful pilgrimage.

Knowledge, keep him in this voyage,
And by that time Good Deeds will be with thee.
But in any wise be siker[27] of mercy,
For your time draweth fast; and ye will saved be,
Ask God mercy, and he will grant truly.
When with the scourge of penance man doth him[28] bind,
The oil of forgiveness then shall he find.

EVERYMAN. Thanked be God for his gracious work!
For now I will my penance begin;
This hath rejoiced and lighted my heart,
Though the knots be painful and hard within.

KNOWLEDGE. Everyman, look your penance that ye fulfil,
What pain that ever it to you be;
And Knowledge shall give you counsel at will
How your account ye shall make clearly.

EVERYMAN. O eternal God, O heavenly figure,
O way of righteousness, O goodly vision,
Which descended down in a virgin pure
Because he would every man redeem,
Which Adam forfeited by his disobedience:
O blessed Godhead, elect and high divine,
Forgive my grievous offence;
Here I cry thee mercy in this presence.
O ghostly treasure, O ransomer and redeemer,
Of all the world hope and conductor,
Mirror of joy, and founder of mercy,
Which enlumineth heaven and earth thereby,
Hear my clamorous complaint, though it late be;
Receive my prayers, of thy benignity;
Though I be a sinner most abominable,
Yet let my name be written in Moses' table.
O Mary, pray to the Maker of all thing,
Me for to help at my ending;
And save me from the power of my enemy,
For Death assaileth me strongly.
And, Lady, that I may by mean of thy prayer

[27]Sure.
[28]Himself.

Of your Son's glory to be partner,
By the means of his passion, I it crave;
I beseech you help my soul to save.
Knowledge, give me the scourge of penance;
My flesh therewith shall give acquittance:
I will now begin, if God give me grace.

KNOWLEDGE. Everyman, God give you time and space!
Thus I bequeath you in the hands of our Saviour;
Now may you make your reckoning sure.

EVERYMAN. In the name of the Holy Trinity,
My body sore punished shall be:
Take this, body, for the sin of the flesh!

[*Scourges himself.*]

Also thou delightest to go gay and fresh,
And in the way of damnation thou did me bring,
Therefore suffer now strokes and punishing.
Now of penance I will wade the water clear,
To save me from purgatory, that sharp fire.

[GOOD DEEDS *rises from the ground.*]

GOOD DEEDS. I thank God, now I can walk and go,
And am delivered of my sickness and woe.
Therefore with Everyman I will go, and not spare;
His good works I will help him to declare.

KNOWLEDGE. Now, Everyman, be merry and glad!
Your Good Deeds cometh now; ye may not be sad.
Now is your Good Deeds whole and sound,
Going upright upon the ground.

EVERYMAN. My heart is light, and shall be evermore;
Now will I smite faster than I did before.

GOOD DEEDS. Everyman, pilgrim, my special friend,
Blessed be thou without end;
For thee is preparate the eternal glory.
Ye have me made whole and sound,
Therefore I will bide by thee in every stound.[29]

EVERYMAN. Welcome, my Good Deeds; now I hear thy voice,

[29]Trial.

I weep for very sweetness of love.
KNOWLEDGE. Be no more sad, but ever rejoice;
God seeth thy living in his throne above.
Put on this garment to thy behoof,[30]
Which is wet with your tears,
Or else before God you may it miss,
When ye to your journey's end come shall.
EVERYMAN. Gentle Knowledge, what do ye it call?
KNOWLEDGE. It is a garment of sorrow:
From pain it will you borrow;
Contrition it is,
That geteth forgiveness;
It pleaseth God passing well.
GOOD DEEDS. Everyman, will you wear it for your heal?
EVERYMAN. Now blessed be Jesu, Mary's Son,
For now have I on true contrition.
And let us go now without tarrying;
Good Deeds, have we clear our reckoning?
GOOD DEEDS. Yea, indeed, I have it here.
EVERYMAN. Then I trust we need not fear;
Now, friends, let us not part in twain.
KNOWLEDGE. Nay, Everyman, that will we not, certain.
GOOD DEEDS. Yet must thou lead with thee
Three persons of great might.
EVERYMAN. Who should they be?
GOOD DEEDS. Discretion and Strength they hight,[31]
And thy Beauty may not abide behind.
KNOWLEDGE. Also ye must call to mind
Your Five Wits as for your counsellors.
GOOD DEEDS. You must have them ready at all hours.
EVERYMAN. How shall I get them hither?
KNOWLEDGE. You must call them all together,
And they will hear you incontinent.[32]
EVERYMAN. My friends, come hither and be present,
Discretion, Strength, my Five Wits, and Beauty.

[30]Behalf, advantage.
[31]THEY HIGHT—They are called.
[32]Immediately.

[*Enter* BEAUTY, STRENGTH, DISCRETION, *and* FIVE WITS.]

BEAUTY. Here at your will we be all ready.
What will ye that we should do?
GOOD DEEDS. That ye would with Everyman go,
And help him in his pilgrimage.
Advise you, will ye with him or not in that voyage?
STRENGTH. We will bring him all thither,
To his help and comfort, ye may believe me.
DISCRETION. So will we go with him all together.
EVERYMAN. Almighty God, lofed[33] may thou be!
I give thee laud that I have hither brought
Strength, Discretion, Beauty, and Five Wits, lack
I nought.
And my Good Deeds, with Knowledge clear,
All be in my company at my will here;
I desire no more to my business.
STRENGTH. And I, Strength, will by you stand in
distress,
Though thou would in battle fight on the ground.
FIVE WITS. And though it were through the world
round,
We will not depart for sweet ne sour.
BEAUTY. No more will I unto death's hour,
Whatsoever thereof befall.
DISCRETION. Everyman, advise you first of all;
Go with a good advisement and deliberation.
We all give you virtuous monition[34]
That all shall be well.
EVERYMAN. My friends, harken what I will tell:
I pray God reward you in his heavenly sphere.
Now harken, all that be here,
For I will make my testament
Here before you all present:
In alms half my good I will give with my hands twain
In the way of charity, with good intent,
And the other half still shall remain

[33]Praised.
[34]Forewarning.

In queth,[35] to be returned there it ought to be,
This I do in despite of the fiend of hell,
To go quit out of his peril
Ever after and this day.

KNOWLEDGE. Everyman, harken what I say:
Go to priesthood, I you advise,
And receive of him in any wise
The holy sacrament and ointment together.
Then shortly see ye turn again hither;
We will all abide you here.

FIVE WITS. Yea, Everyman, hie you that ye ready were.
There is no emperor, king, duke, ne baron,
That of God hath commission
As hath the least priest in the world being;
For of the blessed sacraments pure and benign
He beareth the keys, and thereof hath the cure
For man's redemption—it is ever sure—
Which God for our soul's medicine
Gave us out of his heart with great pine.
Here in this transitory life, for thee and me,
The blessed sacraments seven there be:
Baptism, confirmation, with priesthood good,
And the sacrament of God's precious flesh and blood,
Marriage, the holy extreme unction, and penance;
These seven be good to have in remembrance,
Gracious sacraments of high divinity.

EVERYMAN. Fain would I receive that holy body,
And meekly to my ghostly father I will go.

FIVE WITS. Everyman, that is the best that ye can do.
God will you to salvation bring,
For priesthood exceedeth all other thing:
To us Holy Scripture they do teach,
And converteth man from sin heaven to reach;
God hath to them more power given
Than to any angel that is in heaven.
With five words he may consecrate
God's body in flesh and blood to make,

[35]Bequest.

And handleth his Maker between his hands.
The priest bindeth and unbindeth all bands,
Both in earth and in heaven.
Thou ministers all the sacraments seven;
Though we kissed thy feet, thou were worthy;
Thou art surgeon that cureth sin deadly:
No remedy we find under God
But all only priesthood.
Everyman, God gave priests that dignity,
And setteth them in his stead among us to be;
Thus be they above angels in degree.

[EVERYMAN *goes to the priest to receive the last sacraments.*]

KNOWLEDGE. If priests be good, it is so, surely.
But when Jesus hanged on the cross with great smart,
There he gave out of his blessed heart
The same sacrament in great torment:
He sold them not to us, that Lord omnipotent.
Therefore Saint Peter the apostle doth say
That Jesu's curse hath all they
Which God their Saviour do buy or sell,
Or they for any money do take or tell.[36]
Sinful priests giveth the sinners example bad;
Their children sitteth by other men's fires, I have heard;
And some haunteth women's company
With unclean life, as lusts of lechery:
These be with sin made blind.
FIVE WITS. I trust to God no such may we find;
Therefore let us priesthood honour,
And follow their doctrine for our soul's succour.
We be their sheep, and they shepherds be
By whom we all be kept in surety.
Peace, for yonder I see Everyman come,
Which hath made true satisfaction.
GOOD DEEDS. Methink it is he indeed.

[*Re-enter* EVERYMAN.]

[36]Count out, pay.

EVERYMAN. Now Jesu be your alder speed![37]
I have received the sacrament for my redemption,
And then mine extreme unction:
Blessed be all they that counselled me to take it!
And now, friends, let us go without longer respite;
I thank God that ye have tarried so long.
Now set each of you on this rood your hand,
And shortly follow me:
I go before there I would be; God be our guide!
STRENGTH. Everyman, we will not from you go
Till ye have done this voyage long.
DISCRETION. I, Discretion, will bide by you also.
KNOWLEDGE. And though this pilgrimage be never so strong,
I will never part you fro.
STRENGTH. Everyman, I will be as sure by thee
As ever I did by Judas Maccabee.[38]

[EVERYMAN *comes to his grave.*]

EVERYMAN. Alas, I am so faint I may not stand;
My limbs under me doth fold.
Friends, let us not turn again to this land,
Not for all the world's gold;
For into this cave must I creep
And turn to earth, and there to sleep.
BEAUTY. What, into this grave? Alas!
EVERYMAN. Yea, there shall ye consume, more and less.
BEAUTY. And what, should I smother here?
EVERYMAN. Yea, by my faith, and never more appear.
In this world live no more we shall,
But in heaven before the highest Lord of all.
BEAUTY. I cross out all this; adieu, by Saint John!
I take my cap in my lap,[39] and am gone.
EVERYMAN. What, Beauty, whither will ye?

[37]ALDER SPEED—Helper of you all.
[38]Judas Machabeus, warrior-king; see Machabees I, chapter 3, of the Apocrypha.
[39]I take my cap off to you so low that it is in my lap.

BEAUTY. Peace, I am deaf; I look not behind me,
Not and thou wouldest give me all the gold in thy chest.

[*Exit* BEAUTY.]

EVERYMAN. Alas, whereto may I trust?
Beauty goeth fast away from me;
She promised with me to live and die.
STRENGTH. Everyman, I will thee also forsake and deny;
Thy game liketh me not at all.
EVERYMAN. Why, then, ye will forsake me all?
Sweet Strength, tarry a little space.
STRENGTH. Nay, sir, by the rood of grace!
I will hie me from thee fast,
Though thou weep till thy heart to-brast.[40]
EVERYMAN. Ye would ever bide by me, ye said.
STRENGTH. Yea, I have you far enough conveyed.
Ye be old enough, I understand,
Your pilgrimage to take on hand;
I repent me that I hither came.
EVERYMAN. Strength, you to displease I am to blame;
Yet promise is debt, this ye well wot.
STRENGTH. In faith, I care not.
Thou art but a fool to complain;
You spend your speech and waste your brain.
Go thrust thee into the ground! [*Exit* STRENGTH.]
EVERYMAN. I had wend surer I should you have found.
He that trusteth in his Strength
She him deceiveth at the length.
Both Strength and Beauty forsaketh me;
Yet they promised me fair and lovingly.
DISCRETION. Everyman, I will after Strength be gone;
As for me, I will leave you alone.
EVERYMAN. Why, Discretion, will ye forsake me?
DISCRETION. Yea, in faith, I will go from thee,
For when Strength goeth before
I follow after evermore.

[40]Breaks.

EVERYMAN. Yet, I pray thee, for the love of the Trinity,
Look in my grave once piteously.
DISCRETION. Nay, so nigh will I not come;
Farewell, every one! [*Exit* DISCRETION.]
EVERYMAN. O, all thing faileth, save God alone—
Beauty, Strength, and Discretion;
For when Death bloweth his blast,
They all run from me full fast.
FIVE WITS. Everyman, my leave now of thee I take;
I will follow the other, for here I thee forsake.
EVERYMAN. Alas, then may I wail and weep,
For I took you for my best friend.
FIVE WITS. I will no longer thee keep;
Now farewell, and there an end. [*Exit* FIVE WITS.]
EVERYMAN. O Jesu, help! All hath forsaken me.
GOOD DEEDS. Nay, Everyman; I will bide with thee.
I will not forsake thee indeed;
Thou shalt find me a good friend at need.
EVERYMAN. Gramercy, Good Deeds! Now may
I true friends see.
They have forsaken me, every one;
I loved them better than my Good Deeds alone.
Knowledge, will ye forsake me also?
KNOWLEDGE. Yea, Everyman, when ye to Death shall
go;
But not yet, for no manner of danger.
EVERYMAN. Gramercy, Knowledge, with all my heart.
KNOWLEDGE. Nay, yet I will not from hence depart
Till I see where ye shall become.
EVERYMAN. Methink, alas, that I must be gone
To make my reckoning and my debts pay,
For I see my time is nigh spent away.
Take example, all ye that this do hear or see,
How they that I loved best do forsake me,
Except my Good Deeds that bideth truly.
GOOD DEEDS. All earthly things is but vanity:
Beauty, Strength, and Discretion do man forsake,
Foolish friends, and kinsmen, that fair spake—
All fleeth save Good Deeds, and that am I.

EVERYMAN. Have mercy on me, God most mighty;
And stand by me, thou mother and maid, holy Mary.
GOOD DEEDS. Fear not; I will speak for thee.
EVERYMAN. Here I cry God mercy.
GOOD DEEDS. Short our end, and minish our pain;[41]
Let us go and never come again.
EVERYMAN. Into thy hands, Lord, my soul I commend;
Receive it, Lord, that it be not lost.
As thou me boughtest, so me defend,
And save me from the fiend's boast,
That I may appear with that blessed host
That shall be saved at the day of doom.
In manus tuas, of mights most
For ever, *commendo spiritum meum.*[42]

[*He sinks into his grave.*]

KNOWLEDGE. Now hath he suffered that we all shall endure;
The Good Deeds shall make all sure.
Now hath he made ending;
Methinketh that I hear angels sing,
And make great joy and melody
Where Everyman's soul received shall be.
ANGEL. Come, excellent elect spouse, to Jesu!
Hereabove thou shalt go
Because of thy singular virtue.
Now the soul is taken the body fro,
Thy reckoning is crystal-clear.
Now shalt thou into the heavenly sphere,
Unto the which all ye shall come
That liveth well before the day of doom.

[*Enter* DOCTOR.]

DOCTOR. This moral men may have in mind.
Ye hearers, take it of worth,[43] old and young,
And forsake Pride, for he deceiveth you in the end;

[41]Shorten our end and diminish our pain.
[42]*Into thy hands,* O Mighty One, *I commend my spirit,* forever.
[43]Value it.

And remember Beauty, Five Wits, Strength, and
Discretion,
They all at the last do every man forsake,
Save his Good Deeds there doth he take.
But beware, for and they be small
Before God, he hath no help at all;
None excuse may be there for every man.
Alas, how shall he do then?
For after death amends may no man make,
For then mercy and pity doth him forsake.
If his reckoning be not clear when he doth come,
God will say: "*Ite, maledicti, in ignem eternum.*"[44]
And he that hath his account whole and sound,
High in heaven he shall be crowned;
Unto which place God bring us all thither,
That we may live body and soul together.
Thereto help the Trinity!
Amen, say ye, for saint charity.

THUS ENDETH THIS MORAL PLAY OF EVERYMAN

[44]Depart, ye cursed, into everlasting fire (Matt. 25, 41).

For a complete analysis of "Everyman" as drama, see the following questions in the "Dictionary of Questions": 1-5, 7, 11, 15-20, 41-127, 133, 142-157.

PROBLEM QUESTIONS

1. Some critics have claimed that seeds of the courtly manner, later to flower in the concept of knighthood in the Middle English period, are already apparent in Anglo-Saxon literature. Review *Beowulf*, "The Seafarer," and "The Wanderer" for specific points which would support this claim.

2. When chivalry, the medieval system of military privileges governing knights, was first developed it already had a legendary past. The court of Arthur, perhaps Arthur himself, never existed. If it is true that the Arthur stories, like the American Western, represent an ideal in men's minds, what light is cast on the nature of literature?

3. Contrast *Sir Gawain and the Green Knight* and *Beowulf* on the following points: concept of the hero, attitude toward nature, and structure.

4. Compare and contrast the ballads of modern America with the popular ballads of medieval England, and discuss the possibility that some of our ballads may be derived from those of medieval England and Scotland. Point out some of the qualities and themes of contemporary American ballads.

5. Some critics of Chaucer believe the portraits in the Prologue to *The Canterbury Tales* are descriptions of actual people; others have held that they are types: the typical knight, the typical student, the typical nun, and so forth. Which seems more likely? What other possibility is there?

6. Our introduction to this literary period states that Chaucer gives us a vast pageant of medieval life. Enumerate, with supporting material from *The Canterbury Tales*, some of the major aspects of medieval life.

7. On the basis of the descriptions of the pilgrims in the "Prologue" and on the basis of certain lines in the "Clerk's Tale," what do you consider to be Chaucer's attitude toward the church and toward the clergy?

8. How does *Everyman* differ from some of the good contemporary drama with which you are familiar? For what kind of audience was *Everyman* designed?

Preface to the Dictionary of Questions

The "Dictionary of Questions for Understanding Literature" is an organized set of the important questions that can be asked about any work of literature. It will serve throughout the four years of high school as the basic source for the questions that teachers and students will be asking about the literature they read. In view of this long-continued reference to the "Dictionary," it seems reasonable to suppose that you will develop the habit of asking yourself these important questions when you come to read independently of teachers and textbooks.

The *organization* of the questions in the "Dictionary" is simple. You move from your first general impression of a work to classification and a tentative statement of the theme; you then analyze the literary techniques used to express and develop this theme; you conclude with a final evaluation of the work in the light of the earlier steps in the process.

The *purpose* of the "Dictionary of Questions" is simply to teach habits of critical reading. It is devised to help you form those habits which will serve you in whatever reading you will have to do. Such habits will enable you to read more intelligently and critically anything from the daily newspaper or reports of a business meeting to the latest significant novel or play. They will help you formulate and express what would otherwise be vague feelings of satisfaction with a significant novel or general feelings of disappointment with a silly movie. In short, the purpose of the "Dictionary of Questions" is to accustom you to ask yourself the important questions you must answer if you are to evaluate properly whatever you read.

The following comments about each of the seven steps will give a quick overall view of the "Dictionary."

The *First View* elicits your first and perhaps superficial reaction after reading the work. In this View you try to familiarize yourself with the piece and begin to express your thoughts on it. The *Second View* asks you to classify the work among the various types of literature, a necessary step before any further analysis can take place. In the *Third View* you are asked a few general questions which will help you to state, at least in rough preliminary form, the theme of the work.

The *Fourth View* contains a series of questions which help you determine the overall structure of the work and the function each of its major divisions has in developing the theme. The *Fifth View*, which contains more than half of the questions in the "Dictionary," seeks a more detailed analysis of such points as style, imagery, figures of speech, characterization and plotting, and so forth. You will find in this View large blocks of questions relating specifically to lyric poetry, fiction, the drama, the film, television productions, and so forth.

The *Sixth View* contains questions about areas outside the work—history and biography, for example—which will help you to understand the work further and relate it to the culture that produced its author.

The *Seventh View*, the last one, offers questions for a final evaluation of the work in terms of comparison with other works and according to your own philosophy of life.

It would be an impossibly large task if all questions were to be asked of each work. There is a core of questions which will apply to any work of literature; but many questions are clearly labeled as applying only to one or other of the literary genres. Therefore, many of the 157 questions are eliminated early, when you decide (in the Second View) that the work belongs under one literary type rather than another.

The following consideration also reduces the number of questions that can be asked about any particular piece. Let us suppose that the work to be analyzed is a rather abstract essay. In that case you would skip over the questions relating to imagery and figures of speech, and concentrate more on those questions which analyze the thought processes and evaluate the moral and intellectual issues. On the other hand, if the poem is a simple lyric, the opposite will be true. There may be very little moral or philosophical content to the poem, whereas the imagery and figures will be the all-important carriers of the author's emotion. Summarily, not all 157 questions *can* be asked of every literary work.

SUMMARY OUTLINE OF THE DICTIONARY OF QUESTIONS

1. FIRST VIEW: **What is my first impression of the work as a total unit?** (Ques. 1)
2. SECOND VIEW: **Under which literary type would I classify the work from a first reading?** (Ques. 2-10)
3. THIRD VIEW: **What is my tentative expression of the *theme* of the work at this point?** (Ques. 11-20)
4. FOURTH VIEW: **How in general is the theme developed by the main parts of the work?** (Ques. 21-42)
5. FIFTH VIEW: **How in particular do the theme and its development give meaning to every part of the work?** (Ques. 43-132)
   - A. ***In all works*—by feeling and thought, style, figures of speech and symbols?** (Ques. 44-61)
   - B. ***In poetry*—by imagery, meter, rhyme?** (Ques. 62-72)
   - C. ***In narratives*—by setting, plot, character, point of view?** (Ques. 73-117)
   - D. ***In drama*—by dialogue, gesture, dramatic conventions?** (Ques. 118-127)
   - E. ***In movies and television plays*—by pageantry, camera, editing?** (Ques. 128-132)
6. SIXTH VIEW: **How is the theme further clarified by knowledge of elements outside the work itself, such as the author's life and times?** (Ques. 133-146)
7. SEVENTH VIEW: **What is my final evaluation of the work? How does the work clarify, support, or contradict my own concept of what the "Good Life" is?** (Ques. 147-157)

Dictionary of Questions for Understanding Literature

BY VERNON RULAND

FIRST VIEW

I. **What is my first impression of the work as a total unit?** I must try first to understand rather than to judge, to read the work with an open mind, to approach the author on his own terms no matter how much he might seem at first to differ with me.

SECOND VIEW

II. **Under which type in the following scheme would I classify the work from a first reading? Why?** I must remember, of course, that many works defy simple classification, even after much study. Placing a label on a work is not an end in itself, but merely a temporary decision about the direction my later questions for understanding will have to follow.

A. ***An important preliminary:*** **Does the work stand before me in its original state?** Although the editor's introduction will often answer this question, I must realize my distance from the original work in all my later analysis of this work. An author's vapid style might be merely the translator's; his apparent brevity might be the result of an editor's condensation.

1. **Is the work before me in its original language, or is it a translation or "modernization" of the original? If a translation, is it an adequate one?**
2. **Is my copy a "revised student edition" or an adaptation from which passages have been omitted? Is it an abridgement, a "Digest"?**
3. **Is this work a chapter or excerpt from a complete work?**
4. **Is this work meant primarily to be read, or to be heard as a poem read aloud and interpreted, or to be heard and seen as a drama in a stage performance?** Perhaps the work was written for an open Elizabethan stage, and loses much of its effect on our contemporary stage.
5. **Is the present edition of the work accurate and trustworthy? What influence do its format, print, and illustrations exert on my analysis of the original work?**

1 2 3 4 5 6 7 8

B. **Is the *complete* work before me *nonimaginative* (nonfiction prose) or *imaginative* (prose fiction or poetry)?** In *nonimaginative works* (*nonfiction*) the author records and reports as scientist, scholar, historian, biographer: he
9 develops already existing material and aims for factual accuracy in his work. In *imaginative works* (*prose fiction* or *poetry*) the author creates a world of his own; he forms his experience into an artistic whole that is more properly called a work of literature than is the nonfictional work.

C. **Under what more specific heading is the work best classified?**

TYPES OF LITERATURE

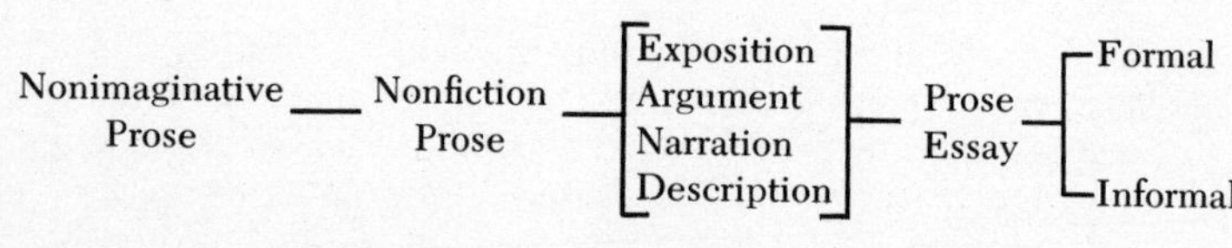

10

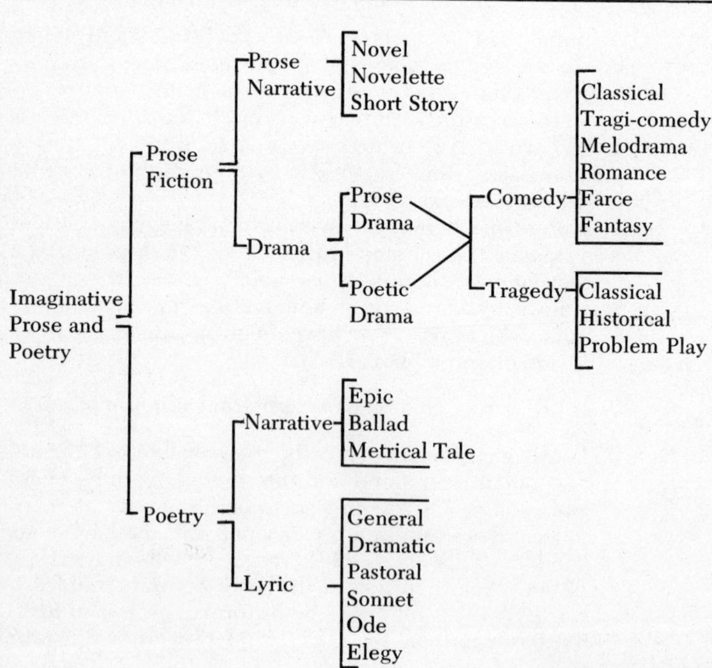

THIRD VIEW

III. **What is the theme of the work?** The theme of any work, best stated in a declarative sentence, is the essential meaning of the subject matter; it is the author's judgment about or attitude towards his subject matter. Any expression of a theme is correct that can justify itself from evidence in the work. Trying to state the theme of a work is *not* an effort to extract a moral or lesson from the work, nor should my statement be so final that it cannot be modified or enriched by further understanding.

With the work already classified in my Second View, the following chart determines my choice of questions for the Third, Fourth, and Fifth Views. Answers to all questions are no stronger than the evidence quoted from the work to support them.

Type of Literature	*3rd View*	*4th View*	*5th View*
I. Nonimaginative Prose (or Nonfiction Prose)	Questions		
A. Exposition	12-14	22-31	44-61
B. Argument	12-14	22-31	44-61
C. Narration	15-20	22-31, 35-42	44-61, (73-117)
D. Description	12-14	22-31, 32-34	44-61
II. Imaginative Prose & Poetry			
A. Prose Fiction	15-20	35-42	44-61
1. Prose Narrative	15-20	35-42	73-117
2. Drama	15-20	35-42	44-61, 73-117, 118-127
3. (Movie & Television Drama)	15-20	35-42	44-61, 73-117, 118-127, 128-132
B. Poetry	15-20	35-42	44-61, 62-72, 73-117, 118-127
1. Narrative Poetry	15-20	(32-34) 35-42	44-61, 62-72, 73-117
2. Lyric Poetry	12-14	32-34	44-61, 62-72

A. *Questions for a Nonnarrative Work (12-14)*

12 1. **What in the subject matter causes the author to feel as he does—entranced, aloof, etc.? Or**

13 2. **Why is the subject matter important to the author? What does it mean to him? Or**

14 3. **What new insight into man and his world does the work seem most concerned about?**

B. *Questions for a Narrative Work (15-20)*

15 1. **What does the author want me to generalize about the central character(s)?**

16 a. **First, who is the central character?**

17 b. **Next, what of major importance happened to him?** (State the importance of the event in a declarative sentence with the central character(s) as subject.)

18 c. **Finally, is it probable that the author wants me to extend my preceding statement to "all men"; or to "every man in such a situation"?**

19 2. **Or what important change or revelation occurred in the central character(s)?**

20 3. **Or what new or significant vision of the world did I grasp through the eyes of the central character(s)?**

FOURTH VIEW

21 IV. **How in general does the theme give order to the whole work?**

A. *Questions for All Nonimaginative Prose (22-31)*

22 1. **If the work is book-length, how does the theme of each chapter develop the theme of the whole book?**

23 a. **What is the theme of the whole book? What chapter best expresses it?**

24 b. **What is the theme of each chapter?**

25 2. **If the work is a reasonably short essay, how is its theme developed?**

26 a. **What is the topic paragraph?**

27 b. **What overall pattern or method best explains how the remaining paragraphs develop the topic paragraph? E.g., enumeration, cause and effect, comparison and contrast, circumstances, examples, repetition, etc.**

28 c. **How does each paragraph fit into this unified scheme?**

**d. What method of *coherence* best explains the con-
nection between successive paragraphs in this** 29
essay?

e. By what method(s) of *emphasis* does the essay give 30
importance to the topic paragraph?

**3. In the development of any given paragraph, how does
the author achieve unity, coherence, emphasis, variety?** 31
How effective is the topic sentence?

B. Questions for Descriptive Prose and Lyric Poetry (32-34)

1. What in the work is the dominant physical *viewpoint* 32
and the mental *viewpoint* (the author's attitude towards
what he describes—sympathetic, ironic, casual, hostile,
etc.)?

2. Record any **noticeable shift from one physical** or
**mental viewpoint to another, from one sense-appeal
to another, from one emotional state to another. How** 33
**do the theme and its method of development explain
these changes?**

**3. If the work is a poem, do differing emotional states
succeed one another and mark the poem into divisions? Does the poet use stanza divisions to mark** 34
**changes in feelings and viewpoints, or does the theme
develop independently of such divisions?**

C. Questions for All Narratives (35-42) 35

**1. What events or historical incidents are handled in each
chapter of the book, or each scene and act of the drama?**

**2. If the work is biography, what important facts and
judgments about the subject's life fall into the following time-divisions: (a) his cultural and family background, (b) his youth, (c) his education, (d) his maturity,** 36
**(e) his decline, (f) his death, (g) a general analysis of
his personality, (h) his achievements, and his effect
on his own and later generations?**

3. If the work is history, what important data belongs 37
to one or more of the following convenient divisions?

**a. Year-by-year, or century-by-century, or term-by-
term of kingship or presidency or in terms of some** 38
characteristic hero of the period?

b. The data pertinent to the history of one nation, 39
then another?

c. Subject-by-subject—the data of religious impor- 40
tance, then political, cultural, economic, etc.?

4. **If the work is prose fiction or narrative poetry, can I divide the material to indicate the growth and release of tension according to the following graph?**

Climax

41 Complication — Resolution

Exposition — Conclusion

5. **Similarly, if the work is tragedy—drama or nondrama—can I construct a graph giving the exposition, rising action, climax, falling action, and catastrophe?**
42 **What are the various inciting forces to account for the hero's rising action, the tragic forces accounting for the hero's falling action, the turning point in the climax, etc.?**

FIFTH VIEW

43 V. **How in particular do the theme and its development give meaning to every part of the work?**

A. *Questions for Understanding All Works (44-61)*

44 1. **What feeling and thought does the work evoke?**

a. **What emotions dominate the work—as signified in my expression of the theme? What emotions stand**
45 **out in each division of the work—stanza or paragraph, for example—and how do they harmonize with the dominant feeling of the entire work?**

b. **Are such emotions as strong as the subject matter**
46 **and theme warrant, or are they excessive or deficient?**

c. **Does the theme in any way so contradict my basic beliefs and convictions about man and the world, and man's place in the world, that I am hindered**
47 **partially or entirely from sharing the feelings of the work? Or does it strengthen my beliefs and increase my sympathy for the work?**

48 2. **How does the author's general style contribute to the development of the theme?**

a. **What does the style tell me about the author's**
49 **personality, and about the social caste, age group, and mentality of his audience?**

50 b. **Are there qualities in the style that appear to be an aid or liability in developing the theme? Why?**

c. **Is the style on a consistent level throughout the**
51 **work, or does it shift to a higher or lower level of expression?**

d. **Is the diction clear, simple, fresh, intense, subtle,**
52 **purposeful; or labored, self-conscious, hackneyed, etc.?**

**e. In expository and argumentative literature, is the logic lucid, mature? Does the author appeal to in-
tellect and feelings both, or strictly to the intellect?** 53
Does he indulge in "loaded language" and in the other common fallacies of false argument?

**3. Why does the author prefer the denotations and con-
notations of one word rather than those of another in** 54
developing his theme?

**a. What does the dictionary record as the exact logical
definition, the pronunciation, syllabification, and** 55
etymology of the word?

**b. Assuming that the author chooses each word intelligently, preferring it to various synonyms, how does
the meaning of any particular word affect a given** 56
context?

**4. How does the author's use of figurative language and
symbols affect the development of the theme?** 57

**a. *Figures of speech*—What is their contribution to the
theme?** 58

(1) Do I recognize the following figures of speech?

(a) *Simile*—expressed comparison with "like" or "as"—"They went by like a jet."

(b) *Metaphor*—implied comparison—"a snowball development" or "He has a thin jackal face."

(c) *Personification*—giving human qualities to the nonhuman—"Death dropped in for a visit."

(d) *Synecdoche*—part designates whole, whole a part—"All hands on deck!" *Metonymy*—word designates an associated relation—"I read Blake."

(e) *Irony*—intended meaning is opposite of 59
literal word-meaning—"I just love to lose a fight!"

(f) *Hyperbole*—exaggeration for effect—"a night of pure hell."

(g) *Litotes*—understatement for effect—"I finished the delicate little snack of five hamburgers."

(h) *Paradox*—an apparent contradiction which is true upon examination—"We must die in order to live."

(i) *Apostrophe*—words spoken in direct address to some abstract quality or nonexistent person—"Sing, Heavenly Muse! that on the secret top of Oreb . . ."

(2) **Once identified, is each particular figure of**
60 **speech fresh and effective? If a literal prose**
statement were substituted in this passage for
the figure, what values would be added or lost?

b. ***Symbols***—(A *symbol* is a word, person, action, or
object which takes on a meaning in the work far
beyond its ordinary meaning; allegory, fable, par-
61 able, and symbol are all extended metaphors.)
What is their contribution to the theme? Is there
any central symbol or metaphor that gives organic
unity and life to the work?

B. Questions for Understanding Poetry (62-72)

1. Any short passage of a poem demands careful study of
word denotations and connotations, figures of speech,
symbols; turning complex grammatical constructions
62 into normal word order; explaining difficult allusions.
Once these preliminaries are finished, the most important questions remain: **Why did the author use this**
word or image or technique rather than another? What
is the relationship between this brief passage analyzed
on one hand—and on the other, the theme and the
dominant feeling of the entire poem?

2. **How does the imagery of the poem contribute to the**
63 **shaping of the theme? Does the imagery unify the**
poem or merely enrich it as an ornament?

64 a. **How varied and sharp is the appeal to each of the**
five senses?

b. **What are the areas of experience that provide the**
65 **sources for the metaphors, similes, and allusions**
in the poem?

3. **How does the metrical pattern of the poem help shape**
66 **the meaning of a particular passage or the total mean-**
ing of the poem?

a. **How closely can I describe the general metrical**
pattern? The four common *poetic feet* are:

Iambic (∪/)—"With wh́at | Ĭ móst | enjóy | cŏn-
teń- | tĕd leást."

Trochaic (/∪)—"Laḱe aňd | rí-vĕr | bréak ă- | sún-
dĕr."

67 Dactylic (/∪∪)—"Whére iš mў | lovělў oňe | wheŕe
iš mў | lovělieš t"?

Anapestic (∪∪/)—"Aňd thĕ míght | ŏf thĕ Gén- |
tĭle, ŭn-smóte | bў thĕ swórd."

A verse of one foot is monometer, two is dimeter,
three is trimeter, four is tetrameter, five is pen-
tameter, six is hexameter, seven is heptameter, eight
is octameter.

b. **The important question is: How do the tensions and pace of the metrical techniques in this poem contribute to its theme and effect? Would the effect be enhanced or weakened if I were to alter these techniques?** 68

4. **How do rhyme and other audial techniques contribute to the effect of a particular passage or the entire poem?** 69

a. **What is the rhyme scheme of the poem?** 70

b. **Is the rhyme scheme conventional to the stanza the poet has chosen? If no rhyme is used, are other audial effects used purposively? E.g.,**

Alliteration—repetition of initial consonants—"brainy but bashful."

Assonance—similar vowel sound in two or more syllables (rhyme is exact in consonant—"wake-take"; assonance is approximate—"wake-fate").

Onomatopoeia—sound of words suggests their meaning—"sizzle" or "screech." 71

Refrain—a phrase or sentence of one or more lines repeated at intervals in a poem, often at the end of a stanza. See Jonson's "Hymn to Cynthia" in which the closing line of each stanza is "Goddess excellently bright."

c. **Are rhyme, meter, imagery, and other techniques used with balanced regularity and variety?** 72

C. *Questions for Understanding All Narratives (73-117)*

1. **If the work is prose fiction or narrative poetry, what is the proportion of dialogue to description and comment? Is the plot cluttered by excessive descriptive detail? Does the story tell itself, or does the author himself intrude to editorialize or moralize?** 73

2. **In a brief paragraph, give a summary of the plot. What incidents are essential to the theme, which merely contributory?** 74

3. **Is the work primarily one of incident and surprise, character problems, or mood and local color; or are plot, character, and setting of equal importance?** 75

4. **How is the setting integrated with the theme?** 76

a. **What are the details of setting?** 77

(1) **The historical period, season, time of day?** 78

(2) **The nation, city, or section of the nation?** 79

80 (3) The social class and occupation of the characters?

81 (4) The mood or atmosphere—tense, gloomy, carefree, etc.?

b. Are these details clearly presented? What is the
82 contribution of the opening sentence to the setting? The closing sentence of the work?

c. What incidents in the story could have happened
83 only in this particular setting; what could have happened at any time or place?

d. If the narrative begins in the middle of events, how
84 does the author provide the reader with sufficient knowledge about characters' past lives and other incidents in order to follow the present story?

85 e. Are later plot changes in time and locality essential to the development of character and plot?

f. Does the environment described in the setting bring such social, economic, political, religious
86 pressures to bear on the lives of the characters that these elements become essential to the shaping of the theme?

87 5. How is the plot integrated with the theme?

a. If the story has a single plot, are any episodes
88 introduced that seem inessential—or even irrelevant—to the theme, characterization, or thread of the story?

b. What conflicts constitute the main action of the story? One emotion or state of mind against another, or one man against another, or man against his physical environment and society—or a combina-
89 tion of these conflicts? How are these conflicts resolved in the work? If unresolved, does some incident in the plot prevent a solution within the work, or does the author apparently want me to leave his work with a problem I must solve for myself?

c. What is the *climax* of the plot, and what bearing does it have on the theme of the work? Does the
90 story end with the climax? If not, would the ending be more effective if the climax came earlier than it does?

d. If there is a *denouement* following the climax, does
91 it attempt to squeeze an obtrusive moral from the story, or does it answer important questions raised in the work, summarize, hint at future events in the characters' lives?

e. ***Foreshadowing and suspense*** **—What is their function in the work?** 92

   (1) **How and with what success does the author employ dramatic foreshadowing and suspense to grip the reader and urge him on to future movements in the story? Does he use *dramatic irony*?** 93

   (2) **If the work has a surprise ending, is the surprise essential to the theme of the story?** 94

f. **Is the plot convincing and plausible? If the work constructs a fantastic world of romance, does it sustain that world throughout the work? If the work strives for realism, on the contrary, is it marred by coincidences improbable in real life?** 95

g. **Are there significant contrasts in the work—between incidents in the plot** (winning the first, losing the second game)? **Between characters** (the vindictive old woman and the congenial doctor)? **Between moods** (carnival gaiety followed by the terror of murder)? **Do these contrasts contribute comic relief, irony, symbolism, or surprise to the total effect of the work?** 96

h. **How does the passage of time function in the plot?** 97

   (1) **Approximately what portion of the story is devoted to exposition, to the complication, to the climax, to the denouement?** 98

   (2) **Does the pace of the story entice the interest of the reader, but still allow sufficient time for plausible character growth and progress of events?** 99

   (3) **Does the plot progress chronologically, or are there skips ahead in time which are later filled in by "flashback" techniques?** 100

6. **How are the characters integrated with the theme?** 101

   a. **Who is the central character in the work? How does the theme evolve out of this character in action? Is the work mainly the story of the central character's development or deterioration?** 102

   b. **What are the dominant traits of the central character?** 103

      (1) **What is significant about his physical appearance, clothes, social status, personal habits?** 104

      (2) **What are the characteristics of his thoughts, speech, and actions?** 105

(3) What is the relation between the character's
106 judgment of himself and the judgment of him
by others?
(4) What is the character's philosophy of life—his
convictions and beliefs about man, the world,
107 and human destiny? Does the author seem
favorably inclined, critical, or noncommittal
towards this philosophy?
108 (5) Do all these character traits harmonize into one
plausible personality?
c. Who are the important subordinate characters?
109 What are their chief traits? Are they distinct personalities, or are they mere surface types?
d. If the work is comedy, what is the exaggerated trait
in the character of the hero or other characters
110 which causes the complications of plot or provokes
comic satire? If the work is tragedy, what personality trait is the "tragic flaw" from which the
catastrophe emerges?
e. Is there real character change during the course of
111 the work, or gradual self-realization and revelation
of hitherto unknown qualities of character?

112 7. From what point of view is the story told?

113 a. Is the narrator the first or third person?

b. If first person, is the narrator an observer only or a
participant in the action? If third person narrator, is
114 the author omniscient—inspecting the most hidden
motives of his characters, trying to keep his own
personality out of the story—or does he tell the story
only from inside the mind of one character?
c. Does the author maintain one consistent point of
115 view throughout the story, or does he change it
during the narrative—and, if so, does he do it
plausibly?
116 d. What advantages and disadvantages result from the
point of view chosen in this particular work?
8. Is it possible throughout the work to sympathize with
the feelings of the central character(s) and the character
117 through whose viewpoint the story is filtered? What in
the work accounts for the ease or difficulty of my
identification with the central character or others?

D. Questions for Understanding Drama (118-132)

118 1. What is the total effect of the play as a combined
venture by author, director, actors, and stage technicians?

   a. How closely does the stage performance achieve 119
   the ideals of the author's original script?
   b. How effectively do author and director employ
   scenery, props, costumes, lighting, make-up, stage- 120
   groupings of characters, exits and entrances, etc.?
   c. What are the names of the actors and the director?
   Are the actors well-cast—in physical appearance, 121
   voice, intelligent interpretation? Do they interact
   well as a unit?
2. How does the work *as a drama* develop its theme in 122
setting, plot, and character?
   a. How does the author respect the limitations and
   exploit the advantages of stage, television, radio,
   etc., in comparison with the novel or short-story 123
   form into which he might have chosen to cast his
   subject matter?
   b. To what extent are the divisions (into scene and act)
   or lack of divisions in the play necessitated by the 124
   medium in which the author is creating?
   c. How effectively do dialogue and gesture accomplish
   what the novelist more readily achieves by simple
   narrative and comment—viz., reveal internal states 125
   of mind, emphasize character differences, speed the
   pace and sustain the interest of the play?
3. How successfully does the author exploit the various
dramatic stage-conventions to accomplish his theme
and effects? E.g., asides and soliloquies, confidants, 126
raisonneur, prologue and epilogue, Greek chorus,
etc.?
4. If *poetic drama*, are the lines good poetry and good
drama both? Do they become at times too reflective
and complex to communicate themselves to an audi- 127
ence that is normally alert and experienced in appreciation of poetic drama?

E. *Questions for Understanding Movies and Television Plays (128-132)*
1. Is the film merely a photographed play that might just 128
as well have been performed in a theater, or does the
camera create a work with unique artistic value in
itself?
2. Give examples of successful camera techniques—
particular close-up studies of a face, fade-outs, etc. 129
What is the effect of each technique on character
portrayal, pace, setting, mood?
3. Does the pageantry of the setting have a value in itself, 130
apart from plot and character?

4. **Has the film been successfully edited to achieve con-
131 tinuity, pace, variety?**
5. **What contribution to the total effect of the work is
made by the sound-track, color, the wide screen, or
other techniques? Is the background music of good
132 independent artistic value, or is it mere sound effects—
muted violins for love scenes and kettle drums for
suspense?**

SIXTH VIEW

VI. **How does my knowledge of elements outside the work con-
133 tribute to further understanding of the work itself?** Study
beyond the limits of the work itself can suggest areas of
scrutiny in the work I might otherwise have overlooked.

A. **How do the author's notebooks, correspondence, and
other comments on his own work shed light on his theme
134 and other elements of the present work? Does this
evidence limit, extend, or merely confirm my present
conclusions?**

135 B. **What light do critical and biographical studies of the
author shed on the meaning of the work?**
1. **Do these studies show me how the present work fits
chronologically into the output of the author's entire
136 career? Do his other works shed further understanding
on this work, and this work shed further understanding
on the others?**
2. **How does the present work agree with or contradict
the author's philosophy of life—both as revealed in
137 the general themes of his works, and as recorded in
other documents?**
3. **Do the author's earlier editions or later revisions of the
138 present work give insight into the meaning of the work?**
4. **How does a knowledge of the sources and analogues of
139 the work contribute to a further understanding?**
a. **Are there people and experiences in the author's
140 own life which bear close resemblance to—or have
directly inspired—people and situations in the work?**
b. **Is the present work an adaptation of another's work,
141 or has the author used his sources creatively?**
5. **How do the individual critic's reactions and inter-
142 pretations of the work add to my understanding of
the work?**

143 C. **How do other bodies of knowledge help me to understand the work?**

1. **How does the knowledge of the history of literature
and the other arts contribute to my understanding of** 144
the work?
2. **How does a knowledge of history and other sciences
contribute to interpreting the work? Was the theme of
the work—and the issues treated—something timely** 145
**when the work first appeared? Are these issues vital
today?**
3. **How does my understanding of the present work, on
the other hand, contribute to an understanding of the
politics, sociology, religion, etc., of the period? How
does it contribute to further understanding of life in
general?** Does the author force me to reëvaluate insti- 146
tutions (marriage, the home, civil law, etc.) and phi-
losophies that I respect? That is, are my ideals re-
affirmed or are they attacked and ridiculed?

SEVENTH VIEW

VII. **What is my final evaluation of the work? How does the work
clarify, support, or contradict my own concept of what the
"Good Life" is?** I have a mental picture, vague or definite,
of what would be for me an ideal life. In determining how
this work of literature affects my idea of this life, I must first
consider what kind of person I am, what kind of person I
should like to be, what kinds of lives I admire, what ideas I 147
respect. I am then concerned about whether the work helps
me to understand my own personality, the character of others,
or the nature of the world. I must consider whether the work
disturbs me because it presents values and sympathies
different from my own, whether it awakens in me a yearning
for a different kind of life, or whether or not it makes me content with my present way of life.

A. **How does a final reading of the work (considering it as a
total unit after all of the analytical study has been completed) compare with my first unanalyzed impressions in** 148
the First View?

B. **Is the development of the theme handled so intelligently
that the work helps me to understand aspects of life
previously confusing and inexplicable to me? Or, on the
other hand, do the theme and important elements in the
work represent, in my judgment, such an immature, distorted philosophy of life that I feel the work to be *artis-*** 149
***tically* inferior?** When I compare the author's theme or
view of a certain aspect of life with my own view, do I
conclude that his notions are not only different from mine
but also so extremely distorted that he has therefore
produced a work of literature which is an artistic failure?

150 C. **How does the theme as it is developed in the work agree with my moral principles?** The following questions pertain chiefly to mature reading-experiences in later life, reading material beyond the scope of the present textbooks.

151 1. **Am I judging the work solely on its own merits, unswayed by the author's known principles and conduct in his private life?**

152 2. **Characters in many realistic works use vulgar, obscene, blasphemous language. Is such language used with artistic purpose for realistic characterization? May it perhaps incite the normal reader to sensual thoughts or immoral behavior?**

153 3. **Are the scenes that describe immorality handled with restraint and artistic distance, and are they a true insight into the nature of immorality?**

154 4. **Is the immorality portrayed in the work presented as *some* type of human evil, or is it presented as the result of social pressures, or as a result of a personality flaw? Does the author recognize immorality as such, even if his characters do not? Moreover, in his work does he punish characters for their immoral behavior—if not, should he have done so? Is the immorality presented as evil only in a certain sense of the word? Is the main conflict in the work between actual moral good and evil, or between what is merely good and bad, pleasant and unpleasant, or socially or politically acceptable and unacceptable, etc.?**

155 5. **Does the work present a set of values so advanced or objectionable that it is to be recommended to mature readers only, or perhaps with a caution to others? Are the scenes or passages to which I object necessary to the artistic integrity of the work, or would the work be seriously mutilated by the omission of such passages?**

156 6. **How does my personal evaluation of the work compare with the judgment of other, more experienced, critics?** In general, are my usual moral evaluations of literature more liberal or conservative—more tolerant or more severe—than their evaluation? In what ways might their conception of the normal reader's problems be more accurate than mine? In what ways less accurate?

157 D. **How does the present work, as I understand it, compare with other works I have read? What difference, if any, is there between the rank I finally assign the work among my favorites, and the objective rank I have assigned it among the world's great pieces of literature?**

Index